When it Rings True
By Josie A. Butler

Giant Publishing Company
Lincoln, Nebraska, USA

2018 by Josie A. Butler

Published by Giant Publishing Company
Post Office Box 6455
Lincoln, NE 68506
www.giantpublishingcompany.com

Printed in the United States of America

Library of Congress Cataloging-in-Publication Data
Butler, Josie A., 1938 -
When it Rings True/Josie A. Butler

TXu 1-899-514
    1. Non-fiction
    2. Autobiographical

ISBN 978-0-9995873-2-4

Cover design by Daniel McQueary

This book is dedicated to the memory of my husband, my hero, Frank (Jack) Butler, a firefighter who lost his life in the line of duty. To my children, grandchildren and great-grandchildren. To my grandson, Shane Butler, who died in a car accident. To my siblings that have passed away in the past four years – Joseph, Antoinette, Anthony, Samuel, and Michael Angelo. And, to my niece, Jackie.

Acknowledgements

I wish to acknowledge and give glory, honor, and thanksgiving to the awesome God Almighty, Jesus Christ, King of kings and Lord of lords. Jesus is the savior of the world, who gave his life for all mankind. Praise and worship God for who he is, for all he did, for all he does for his children, for his loving kindness, and his forgiving mercy.

God bless my family, friends and Publish America for publishing the first true story I ever wrote, titled: *"Heart Of A Victim In Harm's Way and Beyond The Kissing Door."* And, two science fiction fantasy, magical, good-over-evil, family-oriented stories, titled: *"Awesome Adventures of Frankie Stargazer"* and, *"Frankie Stargazer's Ultimate Battle."*

I wrote a screenplay titled: *"Frankie Stargazer and the Power."* I hope that one day it will be produced/developed into a film.

I'd like to thank my family for their love and support - Joe and Shelly, Greg and Renee, Angela and Richard, and Frankie. Love to my grandchildren, Megan and Mike King, Shane, Drenda, Chance, Josie, Joshua, Justin, Jonah and Jessie. Last but not least, I'd like to acknowledge my great-grandchildren, Tobey and Perry.

Thanks to my Angelo family - Joseph, Anthony, Antoinette, Mary, Sam, George, Mike and Frank. Thanks for the daily phone calls from my sweet sister Skeets. Thanks to my friends - Denise, Gail Wilkerson, Soni, Sandy, Mike S. and Cindy Elder.

I'd like to recognize Lydia Cornell, star of "Too Close for Comfort," and Lonnie Senstock, Mario Domina, Brad Binning, Peg and Lew Hunter, and Pam Hunter, my mentor in writing.

Thanks to Saint Elizabeth hospital, to the staff, the nuns and clergy, to the doctors and medical personnel, for the loving care they bestowed on me during cancer treatments.

To Dr. Medathada, Dr. Wiltfong, Dr. Cole, Dr. Jex, Dr. Howell-Burke, Dr. Miller, and Dr. Harris, and to their partners, and to the numerous doctors and nurses at Saint Elizabeth hospital that cared for me and care for others.

A special thanks to my family doctor of twenty years, Dr. Jirovec, who has not only been my doctor, but also been a really good friend.

A special thank you to Daniel McQueary for the wonderful work he did on the cover art design.

I am thankful to be a cancer survivor/warrior who is able to see another sunrise and sunset. I believe God is the great healer. Isaiah 53:5b: "With his stripes we are healed." Thank you, Jesus.

When it Rings True
Memoirs of a Cancer Patient/Survivor/Warrior

Preface

For longer than I can remember, I told myself that nothing more was going to get into my life without my permission. Standing at the front door each time the bell rings, I give everything and everyone a once-over before I open it. But then, cancer was already inside, and I didn't know it.

Of course, that ticked me off. It didn't knock, it didn't ring a bell and it didn't call out. It just walked right in. So, I had a houseguest, and an unwanted one to boot.

So okay, it was in. And I had to do everything I could, and everything anyone else could, to change that. I made up my mind that cancer wasn't going to define me. It was an alien invader and I darn sure wasn't going to let it change me. Little did I know?

When three doctors told me that I had six months to a year to live, I said, "Not on my watch." It could be cancer all it wanted, but it wasn't going to claim me, make me cancer. I wasn't going to let it morph me out of my own existence.

I made a pact with myself to go forward. No matter what happened, I had to keep my eye on the prize. Nothing came easy but I held onto the faith, the belief that God was going to give me the strength to continue to fight the battle and win the war, even when my insides trembled with fear and misgivings.

During the course of my illness I learned that sickness, medicine and treatment affect everyone in different ways. As I talk about my experience it is not to take away from others who have experienced it all in a different manner.

I was determined to 'stay the course.' As I endured the adventure I clung to this scripture: Psalm 139, Verse 16: "Your eyes saw my substance being yet unformed. And in your book they all were written, the days fashioned for me, when as yet there were none of them."

Table of contents

Chapter 1
Seemingly Unreal

I believe in miracles. I'm no one special. Just an ordinary average Joe, or I should say, Josie. I raised four children that grew up to be the greatest accomplishments I could ever hope to achieve. Although today, at this very moment, I feel there is so much more I have to do, so much more I have to say and so little time to say it in.

After all the things I had been through in my lifetime, I thought nothing could harm me anymore. I had been there, done that and thought, holy cow, I've seen it all. I soon changed my mind.

For longer than I can remember, I had believed that nothing more was going to get into my life without my permission. It was like standing at the front door and giving everything and everyone a once-over before opening it. But then, cancer was already inside, and I didn't know it.

Of course, that ticked me off. It didn't knock, it didn't ring a bell, and it didn't call out. It just walked right in. So, I had a houseguest, and an unwanted one to boot.

So okay, it was in. And I had to do everything I could, and everything anyone else could to change that. But until I could get it evicted I made up my mind it wasn't going to define me. It was an invader and I was darn sure it wasn't going to change me.

Even when three doctors told me I had lung, lymph and bladder cancer, that I had six months to a year to live, I said, "Not on my watch." It could be cancer all it wanted, but it wasn't going to make me cancer.

I am who I am, and it wasn't going to morph me out of my own existence. We'd never see eye to eye. I am beautiful; it is ugly. I am a healer; it is a killer. I am a giver; it is a taker.

Oh sure, I sound tough, and I was trying so hard to be positive. Half of me felt courageous, but the other half was scared to death. Talk about ambivalent feelings. Much as I wanted to believe things wouldn't change, that they could remain the same, I was wrong.

There were so many changes to cope with, I didn't know which way to turn. So, I began to make a pact with myself to continue to go forward. No matter what happens, I must keep my eyes on the prize.

It sounds crude, but I've just got to say it, cancer really does stink. No matter how much I tried to act like I was doing okay, my insides always felt like they were trembling. The situations, or maybe I should say the adventures that I was about to embark on threw my family and me into turmoil.

Quite suddenly my life was beginning to feel like I was riding on a merry go round that just wasn't going to stop. There was simply no way to get off.

My children understood that I was trying to cope. What they didn't know was how I began to think of it as a war raging on. Winning one battle, then another cropping up. I kept trying to resign myself to do whatever it took to defeat the enemy. I repeatedly tried to maintain a sense of humor.

I'd always been independent, wanting to do my own thing. I used to say, "If I can't do it, it couldn't be done." Now here I was, leaning heavily on my two daughters, Angela, the eldest, and Frankie, the youngest. They ran me to so many doctors' appointments, to the hospital, clinics and wherever else I needed to go.

They were there for me no matter what came up. They tried so hard to be strong. Nevertheless, I was sure they had thoughts about the subject that they didn't want to share. I don't think they knew when I looked at them that their eyes were saying so many things to my heart.

It was like being in la-la land. Even though cancer treatments were explained to me, there were so many things I didn't understand, along with all that I was about to endure.

During the course of this time, I didn't want to deal with anything. I merely wanted to sleep through the whole day without waking up.

That is exactly what I was reflecting on the day Angela and I were driving down the road at seven-thirty in the morning. We were on our way to the hospital for my first radiation treatment.

We stopped at a McDonald's drive-through and ordered two cups of coffee.

We asked for three creams for each cup and two packages of sugar. We drove up to the window and paid. Then we went to the next window to pick up our order.

I handed Angela her coffee and three creams. I opened the sack and there was one cream container and no sugar. I said, "They forgot the sugar. Oh well, I guess it is okay. I don't really need it. It won't kill me to drink a cup of coffee without sugar."

With a blank look on my face I stared into the steaming hot cup of coffee. I felt like I could see myself in the hot black liquid, clouds of doubt swirling in my brain.

Sugar in my coffee was the least of my worries.

As we drove closer and closer to Saint Elizabeth hospital I was trying to be brave, trying so hard not to think of the task at hand. It wasn't long before we arrived at our destination.

Try as I might, nothing made sense; nothing seemed to matter. Regardless of all the things the doctor told me about the radiation, I repeated the word over and over, "Radiation, what is that really? Is it poison that will permeate my whole being?" The thought of having a foreign substance coursing through my body was horrifying.

Angela was escorting me to the first of forty-four radiation treatments.

To add icing to the cake, I was told that I was to have the radiation treatments and chemotherapy at the same time, along with several different types of surgery. Even though I didn't know exactly what I was in for I took this information to heart. I said, "All right then, if it helps, I could do this."

Then, when I was home alone and wasn't trying to be courageous for myself or anyone else, it felt like I was in a dream, or I should say, a nightmare. There were howling winds blowing my hair in the breeze as I walked down an unknown path. I didn't know where it would lead to, but I knew I had to keep walking.

I'd wonder, where did all my good intentions of being a brave overcomer go? It seemed like I just had those ideas a few seconds ago. My mind jumped from one thought to another faster than a speeding bullet. One minute all was going to be well, the next, I felt like I was falling over a cliff.

I kept telling myself, "Stop it. I am going to be a warrior and beat this cancer. The dreaded disease that was attacking so many people is not going to get the best of me. The best is yet to come."

I still had so much I wanted to do. There were so many places to visit. So many things that I have never seen or done that suddenly became important to me.

I just wasn't ready to leave the face of the earth yet; I especially didn't want to leave my children. Along with two daughters,

Angela and Frankie, I have two sons, Joe and Greg, who both lived out of town.

Joe was my oldest son and he lived in Tennessee. Greg, the second oldest, lived in Kansas. So along with having to work and take care of their own families, they were too far away to join in the hoopla-taking place. They would like to have been here to help but they just weren't able to leave family and business at this time.

I have nine grandchildren and at this moment in time, I have two great-grandchildren. One of my grandchildren, Shane, was twenty years old when he was killed in a terrible car accident two years ago. A shock to the system to lose a child, we continue to endure his loss in sadness. Shane is always and ever on my mind, so much a part of my life and of my story.

We kept the telephone lines busy keeping everyone up to date on my progress.

There was so much more Angela and Frankie had on their shoulders besides getting me from appointment to appointment. They cooked for me, watched over me and took care of me when I was laid up in bed.

They were diligent to stay with me during surgery and all the other times I was hospitalized for days on end.

My son in-law Richard kept his eye on me too and pitched in with all the chores. They all took turns taking care of my big old Shar pei dog.

As Angela and I continued to drive on the busy streets, stopping for red lights, listening to the hum of the tires on the asphalt streets, I recalled the day it all started. It was March 11, 2007.

I was healthy most of my life, except for an occasional cold or the flu. The situations I went to see the doctor for were very minimal. My biggest problem was trying to lose weight and keep it off.

Even being diagnosed with diabetes twelve years ago didn't bother me. I was fortunate that I didn't have to be on insulin. The doctor prescribed a certain pill to keep my blood sugar level down.

So, I continued to do my own thing without giving it another thought. Well, I should say that I did do something on my own, and that is to try to eat more healthfully and keep carbohydrates at a certain level. But having a sweet tooth, sometimes I cheated and ate a donut or a piece of cake, or I should say, whatever struck my fancy.

I never liked talking about my health to anyone, let alone describe what happened. It seems a little gross and disgusting to talk about how it all started but in order to convey the facts, this is the story of what happened the morning I woke up and my world, as I knew it, changed.

And possibly, it may not be as bad as I am making it out to be, but still, a word of warning that at times my story doesn't paint a pretty picture. Just the same, I hope you all stay with me during the description of my dilemma.

Just as I always did, I woke up in the wee hours of the morning to go to the bathroom, which was right next to my bedroom. I rarely turned on the light and just made my way in the dark.

This particular morning, I flicked on the light. Then as I turned to flush the toilet, I gasped aloud. Being sleepy eyed it was a rude awakening. Every inch of the toilet bowl was filled with bright orange red blood. I wondered, What the heck? I didn't even feel sick.

This can't be, it just can't be. Reality hit me and I realized it wasn't a dream; it was real and I had to take action.

I went back into the bedroom, turned on the lamp by my bed, and checked out what time it was. It was four a.m. I didn't care what time it was, I was going to call my family doctor. There was another doctor on duty and he told me to go to the hospital emergency room right away.

I called Angela and said, "Now don't panic or be alarmed but I need to go to the hospital immediately. I'm sorry I had to call and wake you but I'll explain what happened on the way."

Angela and her husband, Richard, and I had bought a duplex together fifteen years ago. They lived in one half and I lived in the other. Living right next door to one another made it easy for us to take about five minutes to get ready, take off and head to the emergency room.

Angela called Frankie to tell her that we were in the hospital and that she would keep her updated on what was happening.

After we were situated in the emergency room and I was in a hospital gown, a nurse came in and told me she needed a urine sample. When I walked out of the bathroom with the sample, Angela nearly fainted when she saw the dark purple color of the urine in the clear plastic container.

I set the container on the ledge and got back on the bed. It was then that I took a really good look at the color in the container. I had to admit, it really looked weird, almost iridescent.

I had a habit of making jokes when I was shaken up. It seemed to ease the tension I felt, as my insides were busy shaking. So, when the nurse came in to pick up the sample, I said, "Doesn't that look like alien pee? If you look closer it's even starting to glow iridescently." She picked up the container and said, "You're right, it looks strange." She walked out of the room laughing.

Angela laughed too. But she had a serious look on her face as she said, "Mom, I've never seen anything like that before." Having worked at Saint Elizabeth hospital for six years, she was familiar with the procedures I was about to undergo.

We were in the emergency room for about a half an hour when the doctor that was on duty said he was leaving. I wanted him to stay and be my doctor. He tried to reassure me as he said, "Don't be worried, one of the doctors on staff will be in soon."

19

Several minutes later a woman doctor came in and checked me over. She said, "You have a bladder infection." She sent me home with a prescription for antibiotics and told me to go see my doctor after the pills were gone.

I wasn't sure what I thought of her diagnosis, but I was thankful when she said that it was just a bladder infection and I could go home.

Chapter 2
The Results

Several days after I started taking the pills, the bleeding stopped, so I thought all was well in my little part of the world. I did what the doctor said and I made an appointment to see my family physician.

A few days later, I went to see Doctor Jirovec. The hospital scanned him the papers with the details of my hospital visit. He asked, "How are you feeling now?"

I said, "The bleeding has stopped. I feel fine so can we postpone the CAT scan test you wanted me to take?"

He was hesitant. Then he excused himself and left the examining room for a minute.

While he was out of the room I needed to walk across the hall and use the bathroom. Lo and behold, the bleeding and blood clots were back flooding the toilet bowl. Yuk!

I walked out of the bathroom. Doctor Jirovec and two nurses were standing in the hallway talking. As I started to walk toward them, they all turned to look at me.

Doctor Jirovec took one look at the scared countenance on my face and he said, "Josie, what's wrong?"

I said, "I'm losing blood again."

The doctor said, "Okay, that's it. You're going to have to do a CAT scan right away so we can see what is going on. Go back into the examining room and wait while we make the arrangements."

The next day, there I was on my way back to the hospital to have the CAT scan to find out what was going on in the lower part of my body. I'd never had one before, so naturally I didn't know what to expect.

I had to drink this awful-tasting stuff that made you feel you were going to explode if you took another sip.

Little did I know that that was going to be the least of my worries for the next two years, or that I would end up having to take many more CAT scans as time went by. But after the first one, I decided that I wasn't going to drink that awful-tasting stuff anymore.

However, I couldn't get out of being injected with the dye they use while they are doing the scan. The dye gave my whole body a warm feeling and a kind of awful taste in my mouth.

So, there I was, lying on the table, about to burst, being injected with dye in my veins. I was claustrophobic, so just the thought of going in any kind of tube waiting to swallow me was a harrowing experience.

The nurses were kind and patient as they assured me that it wouldn't take long. They were right. It was soon over. For the moment, my fears subsided.

I got down off the table, relieved to have it over with. But still, after I left the room I worried that the dye they injected was still within me.

The nurse said, "Now be sure to drink a lot of water."

There it was. Oh my, I was right. That dye was still swishing around and now I had to spend the day washing it out so it wouldn't harden. It is easy to construe that I wasn't fond of medicine in any form.

The highlight of each visit was that Angela liked to treat me every time I went through a procedure, so she'd take me out to lunch. If she had time, some days she'd go to the hospital gift shop and buy me a little trinket and surprise me with it while we were sitting in the restaurant waiting for our food. That was one of my favorite times. Little gifts perk me up.

The next evening, I was home lying in bed watching TV when the phone rang. It was Dr. Jirovec, my family doctor for sixteen years. I had great respect and love for him.

I'm sure he probably had his own bad days here and there, but no matter how he felt he was always kind and thoughtful. He had so much empathy while caring for his patients' well-being. He was one of my favorite people in the whole world.

We said hello and I asked, "What's up Doc? Kind of late for you to be working, isn't it? We made some small talk for a minute. Suddenly his voice became serious and he sounded like he was in the far away distance. I couldn't believe what I was hearing. Just then I had a flashback of our history as doctor and patient.

My family doctor knew me only too well. I was an expert at spacing things off, I tried to get out of every test that they said a woman my age should have. I'm sure I exasperated him at times but he never showed it.

Eventually, I'd give in and have the tests. Even so, it wasn't until the last few years that I finally gave in and started to take a flu shot.

Twelve years ago, after I procrastinated for months on end when I finally agreed to go and get a physical checkup, Dr. Jirovec found a lump in my breast and he sent me to a specialist.

I was a little frightened, but not bad. I was kind of brave back then. Thank God, it turned out to be benign. So, cancer was put on a back burner. I didn't give it another thought.

I considered that being healthy, nothing serious would happen to me. I had a lot of energy and loved doing so many different, daring things. I used to brag about riding the roller coaster situated on the very top of the Stratosphere building in Las Vegas.

My mind flashed back to the present, and as we continued to talk on the phone, all of a sudden, Dr. Jirovec's voice changed. He sounded sad, tear-filled and serious. He went on to say,

"Josie, I'm sorry I had to call you at this time of night. I got the results back from the radiologist today.

"The test shows that you have bladder cancer. That's not the end of it. I'm afraid the radiologist found something else. Just the tip of your lung was showing because the scan was taken on your bladder. It shows that you have a tumor that looks cancerous. You need to go in for more tests. Come in to see me Monday and we'll talk some more and make the necessary arrangements. You'll need to have an oncologist on board, too. I'm so sorry Josie, so very sorry."

I grew quiet, which was a first for me. I was rarely quiet. I always had something to say about everything. I felt thunderstruck.

When I finally got my bearings back I said, "Doctor, I don't know what to say. Your words have taken me by surprise and knocked the wind right out of me. I recognize how hard this must have been for you to call and tell me. Since I'm not sure what to say at this time, I'll just say thanks for calling and for your kindness and sympathy. I'll come in and see you first thing Monday morning. I'll talk to you later; bye Doc."

I don't remember hanging up the phone or crying or anything else. I was in shock. I was off in another world. I don't know whose world it was but it couldn't be mine. It just couldn't. My head was spinning as I walked over to my desk, picked up a pack of cigarettes, took one out of the pack and lit it. Then I went to the kitchen to make a cup of coffee.

I walked slowly back to the bedroom which served as my office, too. I set the coffee cup on my desk, sat in my comfortable desk chair and I turned on the computer.

I taught myself to type on an old used computer and began to write stories. The computer was a piece of junk. It kept freezing and I'd end up losing the material I was working on. I persisted and continued to peck away at the keyboard.

I read certain books to figure out how to get the right format. I looked at the way other writers wrote screenplays. After much trial and error, and a new computer that my son Joe bought me, I became a four-time published author and a screenwriter.

I began to love writing. It felt like I was filling the hours with something that had meaning. It was like a healing therapy.

After contemplating the events of the day, I sat for a while with a cigarette in one hand, coffee in the other. Even though my mind was cluttered I wrote a few sentences. But, the words on the computer screen became a blur. I stopped writing, turned off the computer and stared into space.

When my thoughts in conclusion cleared, all I could think about was how to tell the children. Even though we had a close relationship, it wasn't going to be easy.

My next thought was that I should try to get some sleep and maybe my mind would stop racing ninety miles an hour. So, I put out the cigarette that I was holding. As I was taking the empty coffee cup back to the kitchen my dog, Jack, started barking to go outside. I took him down the stairs, opened the door and let him out one more time before calling it a night. I loved it that Frankie named the dog Jack after my deceased husband.

Waiting for the dog to finish his business I aimlessly stared out the patio door. The moon was full, lighting up the dark night sky. The multitude of stars was twinkling brightly, adding to the beauty of the night. The air smelled fresh and clean.

After several minutes, I called the dog in and headed back up the stairs. Maybe, the dog diverting my attention gave me a burst of energy. I decided to make another cup of coffee and give writing another chance.

I was used to keeping late hours. I liked working in the evening better than the daytime. It was less disturbing. During the day the phone rang off the hook and someone was always knocking on the door. Along with having to run errands all the time, I got in the habit of writing late at night into the early morning hours.

As the clock ticked on, my good intentions to write went by the wayside. Not being able to concentrate, I ended up turning the computer on and off.

I kept hearing the doctor's words over and over, bladder cancer and cancerous tumor on my right lung. What a bummer, cancer in two areas of my body. How could that be? I didn't know yet that there was a third area that was affected too.

The night faded away as I opened the blinds and looked out the window. The sun was rising on the horizon. As the stunning sunlight filtered in the room I noticed the sky was blood orange with yellow streaks.

I listened to the birds singing in the early morning beauty. All seemed normal as the new day brightened the world.

It was Saturday morning and right then and there I decided to wait until Sunday after church to tell the children the news. That gave me a little more time to figure out how to tell them that their mother has cancer.

For some strange reason I didn't like saying the word cancer. But there it was, I said it out loud, cancer, and the rest of the experience is history.

Chapter 3
A peek at the past

I wasn't sure how I was going to get through Saturday devoid of spilling my guts. I was going to try to tell the children in a nonchalant manner without any dramatics. I was gearing up for the worst.

I didn't want them to see how freaked out and upset I really was. So here I was; I had to act like nothing was wrong for the rest of the day.

Frankie usually did the grocery shopping every Saturday morning. It wasn't long before she came walking in the house with her arms loaded down with groceries.

I got in the habit of having her do my shopping at the same time she did hers. I only went to the store with her when I wanted to fix something special, like a roast or a meatloaf. She was a vegetarian and didn't like going by the meat counter.

I went into the kitchen to help her put the groceries away. I said, "Frankie, let's go out for lunch today. My treat. I don't feel like cooking. It's such a beautiful day I feel like going somewhere."

Frankie said, "Mom, can we eat here today? I don't feel like going back out. For some reason traffic is so heavy. Let's just stay home and fix grilled cheese sandwiches."

"Okay, sweetie. That sounds good. We can go out another time." I replied.

We fixed lunch, turned on the TV and just hung out. After about an hour or so I got up and went out on the deck to have a cigarette. Frankie was allergic to smoke and she couldn't stand the smell.

None of my children liked my smoking. They were always on me to quit. I kept telling them that I enjoyed it. It calmed me down when I was nervous and I thought it helped to keep my weight down.

I ignored the warnings about smoking causing cancer. Thinking, I'm a cool person, it won't happen to me. After all, I've heard that people who don't smoke are getting cancer too. I used every excuse out there to deny what cigarettes could do to one's body, and I continued to smoke. I told myself that I could give it up any time. I denied that it was habit forming because I gave up smoking for ten years before taking it back up again. When my husband passed away the first thing I did was buy a package of cigarettes, and there I was hooked again.

I felt it wasn't pleasing to God to smoke, but I even made up excuses about that. I never knew what it meant but I called that a gray area.

Clearly, I was nervous, anxious and overwhelmed. I could not stop thinking about the doctor's phone call and what to tell the children.

I walked out on the deck, sat in the lounge chair, lit a cigarette and watched the smoke as it lingered on and disappeared in the air. I kept telling myself, what did it matter if I smoked? It was relaxing. I wasn't hurting anyone. I know now how stupid that kind of thinking was.

Just then the neighbor lady stepped onto her deck, which was right across from mine, and she lit a cigarette. So, I said to myself, see she is smoking too, so what's the big deal? A lot of people do it.

Once again, my attention wandered back to the children. Even though I was sad, my attention started to drift away from the job at hand. I actually began to enjoy the beauty of the day. We lived behind a really busy street and I started watching the cars zoom by! I pondered on the way they seemed to be in such an all-fire hurry.

After a bit, Frankie opened the patio door and said, "Mom, I'm getting ready to go to my apartment pretty quick. Want to come in and say good-bye?"

I said, "Sure do, wait a second."

I put the cigarette out in the ashtray that I kept on the patio table and walked inside. I hugged and kissed her and said, "See you in the morning, then?"

Frankie sensed something was going on with me as she replied, "Yes, Mom. See you in the morning. Are you sure you're okay? You act like you don't feel well."

31

"I'm feeling fine; I'm just tired. I didn't sleep well last night. Call me when you get home," I said.

She replied, "Okay, I'll call you the moment I walk in the door."

I was good at putting things off but this is one time I couldn't procrastinate. I had to figure out right away how to tell the children. It plagued my mind knowing how hard it was going to be to inform them. It was equally tough keeping it to myself. As I watched Frankie drive down the street I thought of her dad and how much I wished he were alive to help me through this. I was the only parent my children had.

My husband, the children's dad, Jack Butler, died quite suddenly in the line of duty while fighting a horrendous fire. Sixteen years later, it still upset me that he was gone. Without him by my side, I had to face everything alone. Even though the children and I are very close I couldn't shake that feeling. He was my soul mate and I missed him something awful.

After he passed away, my children and I made sure we knew where the other one was at all times. We had a habit of calling one another whenever we went from one place to the other. We called when leaving for work or going home from work or whatever happened to be going on.

It was disturbing to see my husband one minute, and the next minute, I was told he was dead.

Losing his life in the line of duty, everyone called him a hero. Most of the town showed up for the funeral. The front page of the local newspaper read, "Jack Butler had a gentle spirit." Jack deserved to be honored. Then again, he was always our hero. He held our hearts as he constantly showed that his family came first.

When I reflect on Jack, I think of what a kind, wonderful Christian man he was. He was patient and stable. He was the one who took care of everything. I leaned on him so much of the time.

On the other hand, I was flighty and sometimes unpredictable. I thought nothing of leaving the car right where it was if it broke down. I'd wait until he got home from work and tell him where the car was and he'd walk to the place and get it running again.

Once I called Jack at work and asked him, "Would you come home because I see something in the sky that I think is a UFO?" He said, "I can't leave work now. You'll have to deal with it until I can come home. Could just be a balloon. Don't worry, everything is okay."

Not being able to lure him home, I called my good friend Kay, to come over and showed her the silvery metal looking object so very high in the sky.

We both stood there looking dumbfounded through a pair of binoculars. Our imaginations carried us into the science fiction story of the day.

We thought the out-of-the-ordinary object was a flying saucer. It was not moving, but remaining stationary. Then all of sudden, it disappeared from our view.

What do we do now? Do we report it, or wait until our husbands return home and see what they think we should do? Our husbands worked in the same factory so they would be home at the same time.

When it was all said and done we learned that the peculiar object turned out to be a weather balloon. Needless to say, it was a laughing matter.

Sounds impossible but true, Jack never once raised his voice to me. When I irritated him, and I know I did, he would silently leave the room and go putter in the garage or work on the lawn.

I'd peek out the window at him and watch him puttering in the yard. Then I'd feel bad that I argued with him over nothing much.

After a while I would ponder over what happened and realize it wasn't worth arguing about, so I'd apologize to him. He had that kind of effect on people. I didn't want to hurt him, ever. He didn't have to witness that he loved God and Jesus because you could see it in his actions, in his tender spirit. He was always ready to help someone.

I was remembering how that frightful day started out like any other day. Jack had taken our thirteen-year daughter, Frankie, to a music lesson. He picked her up when it was over and brought her back home.

She came in the house alone and started watching wrestling. They both loved wrestling and watched it together once a week like clockwork.

Every so often I made fun of the wrestlers so Frankie and Jack loved it when I'd have to attend a council meeting so they could be home alone to enjoy their show. To this day, she still watches wrestling.

This particular evening, I didn't have a meeting. I went upstairs to the bedroom to watch TV. After a while I went back downstairs.

I asked Frankie, "Where is your dad? Did he just drop you off and go somewhere?"

She said, "I don't think so. When I got out of the van in front of the house, he told me he was going to drive the van into the garage and would be coming in the house pretty quick."

Contemplating what she said, I thought that he might have decided to stay in the garage to work on one of the many projects he'd started. I went back upstairs.

The garage was located in the back of the house by the alley. Pretty soon, I walked out on the back porch several times to see if he was there. But the van blocked my view. Seeing the garage door was open and the lights on, I figured he was puttering at his worktable behind the van. Not wanting to bother him, I turned around and walked back into the house.

I didn't know that the fire radio he wore on his belt went off and he was gone. The fire department stopped blowing the sirens when there was a fire because there were too many spectators showing up and getting in the way of the firefighters. Therefore, I didn't know he had left home in his pickup truck that was parked in the dark alley behind the house. He always took off like a bat out of heck when the fire radio sounded the alarm.

Another hour went by when I walked out onto the porch again and looked out toward the garage. Seeing nothing had changed, I yelled out, "Hey Jack, what are you doing? Are you coming in soon? Can you hear me?"

There was no answer, but I still didn't think anything was amiss.

Noticing that there was no sound coming from the garage, I thought he might have walked over to chitchat with one of our neighbors, and he would be home soon to watch wrestling with Frankie.

Little did I know that he was lying dead in a field near the railroad tracks, as the thick, black, smoky hot prairie fire was raging on.

Just a few minutes had passed since I looked out to see if he was in the garage when a policeman knocked on the door.

When I answered the door the policeman said, "Josie, you have to come to the hospital, there has been an accident."

I said, "What is it?" Shall I bring my daughter with me?"

Not fully understanding the extent of what the officer was telling me I turned to Frankie and said, "Do you want to wait here or come with me?"

Frankie said, "I don't know, what do you want me to do?"

I said, "Why don't you wait here and I'll be right back."

My husband had been injured once before. It wasn't severe so I assumed this was not serious either. I went with the policeman to the hospital, which was just a few blocks from our house. On the way to the hospital, the wind started to pick up and it started to thunder as lightning flashed across the sky and then, it started to rain.

The policeman had not yet told me exactly what was going on or what happened. As we walked in the hospital door the firemen were standing around in the hallway looking at me with sad, wounded eyes.

Being on the city council I knew everyone there so I said, "Hi guys, what is going on? Where is Jack?"

They all stared at me with a look of sadness on their face as the doctor and the fire chief guided me into a small room. The doctor just blurted out, "Your husband is dead."

A blank look came over me, as I said, "No, he can't be dead, I don't want him to be dead."

They steered me into a room where Jack lay on a table, still and unmoving. Oddly enough, he looked peaceful. The sight of him sent me reeling. I got weak in the knees and light headed. I was about to fall as I grabbed the doctor's arm. In the next instant I felt a wheel chair sliding under me and I was being wheeled into another room.

The room was already filled with several relatives and some of the townspeople. We were all crying and carrying on as the telephone in the room continued to ring.

After they told me the news, the policeman went back to my house to get Frankie and bring her to the hospital.

When she walked into the hospital room she came over and stood by my side. There was a look of bewilderment on her face when she saw all the people and her mom crying in the wheel chair. I don't know if I was the one or if someone else told her that her dad had died fighting a fire. We looked stunned as we looked into each other's eyes. She grabbed my hand and held on for dear life. Our world fell to the ground with a booming crash. The hospital called my daughter Angela and son in-law Ritchie and in an instant, they jumped in the car and headed to Marysville, KS, where Jack, Frankie and I lived. At the time, Angela and Ritchie lived in Lincoln, Nebraska.

Angela called her two brothers who lived in California. It wasn't long before they hopped on a plane and arrived in town the next day.

Two days after Jack passed away, my granddaughter Megan became very ill and had to be taken to the hospital. She was seven years old at this time and was very upset about losing her grandpa.

While I was standing in Megan's hospital room, a fireman came in and asked if he could talk to me. I said, "Yes, of course."

Right there in the hospital room he proceeded to tell me that he heard I was going to hire an attorney and sue the city. Here I was in shock over losing my husband, standing in my sick granddaughter's hospital room, and he had the audacity to ask me about a lawsuit. As yet, I had not talked to anyone except my immediate family.

I was astounded that he would approach me to ask such a question. I said, "No, I am not going to sue the city. The thought never entered my mind. My husband loved Marysville and the fire department."

Later I found out why he asked me that question. They were afraid something that occurred the evening of the fire would be brought to light, and eventually it was.

I tried to handle the situation in a manner that covered the city's negligence to have proper equipment for all the firemen to wear when they go out to fight a fire. Up until that time they didn't have enough safety fire masks to go around. Unbelievable that some of the men were fire-fighting wearing paper masks.

I gave the city of Marysville all the memorial money that was collected in Jack's memory. The city matched the funds and bought the equipment needed so that all the firemen would have the kind of gear they require to keep them out of harm's way.

I don't know what brought this incident to mind, for I have not thought of it or spoken of it, up until now. I had not even shared this information with my daughter Frankie. Asking me if I was going to sue added insult to injury.

Although the townspeople spoke highly of Jack in the local newspaper, and a lot of people showed up for the funeral, I was never sure if the city fully appreciated or discovered all that Jack gave of himself for the betterment of the community, which included his life.

Nonetheless, time marches on and people soon forget and gossip runs amok. Sometimes it hurts to go back for a visit and run into someone that has never heard of the only fireman in town that died in the line of duty.

I thought it would be a nice gesture if the city would put a plaque up in the city hall building bearing Jack Butler's name, and what he did for the city, so he is remembered for years to come.

I know I sound emotional. Nevertheless, even if no one else ever feels the way I do, after twenty-two years, it feels good to say it.

I'll forever and always think of Jack as the unsung hero of Marysville, Kansas. A soldier, long forgotten, but whose gentle spirit lives on.

On the other hand, from the moment we heard the unfortunate news about our beloved husband and father, the children and I clung together, tighter than ever to each other. To this day we continue to hold on to one another for dear life.

After all this time, I still grieve for Jack. I think one just learns to live with it and tolerate that their loved one has left the face of the earth to play with the angels.

That was one of my worst days ever, and still is.

On the other hand, no matter how much time has passed since we were married, it still feels like he was only here for a day. I am thankful to the Lord for the time we had together and for watching over my family and me.

Needless to say, though, after he passed away, things changed drastically. Although we learned to cope, we never really got over what happened. It was scary that I had to figure out how to raise a thirteen-year old by myself.

Here I was, grieving and feeling depressed. But for some reason during this time I got it into my head that I would love to be involved in a church where we could worship God freely in spirit and in truth.

After seeing how quickly and unexpectedly someone can pass away, I wanted a pastor to reach out and teach the salvation message. A pastor once told me a church that is alive is worth the drive.

My friend, Denise had the same vision that I had. We decided to take a step out in faith. That meant we had to leave our comfort zone. There were just a few of us but we began to meet on Sunday mornings in my home.

Now then, I'm not saying we didn't have churches in town that were doing this very thing. The town had some beautiful churches. Their services were done in the traditional manner that they had been doing for years and years. They were kind, loving people and we loved them.

It made a few people irate when they found out we were meeting in my home.

Someone called me on the telephone and said, "Josie, why are you doing this? We have a church right here that is serving and worshipping God."

I said, "I am not trying to hurt or undermine anyone. If this is from God then it will work, if it is not from God then it will not work. Let's wait and see what happens."

In my heart I felt the Lord was doing a new thing. I was thankful to be a part of it. Denise's husband Steve supported our vision and endeavors.

And then it happened. My friend Denise and I actually did it. Along with meeting in my home on Sunday mornings we played our guitars and we worshipped together and then we had a Bible teaching.

We encouraged my son and his wife, Joe and Shelly, to come be a part of what we were trying to accomplish and do the teaching. Joe and Shelly had attended North Central Bible College, and he was a wonderful teacher. They came and Joe taught the Sunday morning service. After the service we all enjoyed fellowshipping and eating lunch together.

It was a great time of sharing God's word in a simplistic manner, filled with love and hope. Throwing myself into this adventure helped me to cope with the grief I felt in losing my husband.

I'm telling you this story so I can write about a phenomenon that took place at one of our Sunday services.

Denise and I used to practice playing guitar and singing praise and worship songs for hours on end. During the 'Desert Storm War' I got it into my head to write some lyrics and songs titled 'American Hero.' I called Denise and asked her to come over and help me record the songs on a cassette tape. The technology of the day was to own a cassette player. So, one day she came over and I sat down at the piano and played the tune as we both sang the songs I wrote.

We decided to send several of the tapes to one of the generals to give to the soldiers. We thought this was our contribution to the war effort. I wasn't a professional musician, nor had any training. I simply taught myself to play guitar and piano and sang with my heart. I loved music.

One morning, as we were getting ready to start our Sunday service, the door opened and in came a new couple that had just moved up the street from me. We welcomed them and they sat down. Denise and I started playing and singing worship songs. When we were done singing the young man who was a stranger that we had never seen before said, "Oh wow, do you realize that I know who you people are? When I was overseas on patrol fighting in the desert someone gave me a tape with your voices on it. I played it over and over until my cassette player messed up from the sand that got into our equipment."

What are the odds of something like this happening? Needless to say, we were flabbergasted. We were so thankful to God for letting us be a part of this young man's life and being able to witness the power of God's grace. We believe this was not a coincidence, but a gift from God. Our God is an awesome God. To get on with the story, I ended up calling the Assemblies of God headquarters and asked them to tell us how to get started in our quest to have a pastor and a church. At first, they said there weren't enough people in the area and that they liked to go into big cities.

With Denise's encouragement, I was persistent and continued to call and talk with the head honcho. In a matter of a few phone calls they started to be encouraging. They seemed to respond to the fact that I told them it shouldn't matter if we were a small rural community; people in small areas need churches just as bad as those in the big cities.

The head of the Assemblies of God finally came to visit us during our Sunday service, and after that they began to send a different pastor to my home every Sunday.

At first, there was only around seven of us that met in my home, but we began to grow as new people were coming into the fold. So, we rented a small building to meet in.

After we grew some more, we got the opportunity to vote on having a permanent pastor take over and we began to rent an Episcopal church.

From the get-go I felt God was guiding us. Although I was sad about Jack, I started to look back at this era as one of the better times.

My daughter didn't feel the same way I did. Thirteen years old was just too young to have to deal with the loss of her father that she loved so much.

Her father had been gone for a year and Frankie was still very unhappy living in the town where he had died. She wanted to move to Lincoln, Nebraska where her sister lived. I wasn't sure if I wanted to move, but I did it for her.

Someone asked me, "Are you going to listen to a thirteen-year-old and move from your home town?"

I said, "Yes I am."

On the other hand, at the time I did wonder how I was ever going to leave the church I had come to love. But I did, and we are still living in Lincoln.

The good news of the "Marysville Christian Fellowship Church" we helped establish is that they purchased twenty-five acres of prime land on the highway and built a beautiful new church building.

The pastor we voted on stayed for around twenty years and then decided to take a position in another state. The church brought in a new pastor, whom I have heard is leading people to Jesus. At this point the congregation has grown to around 200.

I thought of the experience as a gift from God and part of my destiny. I had almost forgotten this important saga of my life. I kind of hesitated to write about it for fear it would turn people off. I wrote about it not to make myself outstanding but to say, 'God can use us wherever we are and when we are at our lowest point.' God plants the seed and someone comes along and waters it until it is ripe for harvest.

Suddenly, just like that, my thoughts flew back to the present time. I felt as if a bolt of lightning came down from the sky and struck me as I stopped daydreaming. I continued to watch

Frankie drive out of sight. I went back out on the deck. My dog followed me and sat by my feet.

Words began swirling around in my fogged-up head and still, I didn't know how to approach the subject with my family.

Nothing seemed real. I had to get my head out of the clouds and realize this dilemma is real. It is, in fact, reality. Whether I liked it or not, somehow or another I had to deal with it. I had to figure out just how to tell them. Then I wondered if there was a right or a wrong way to tell them.

I called Angela and Ritchie and asked if they would be able to get together with Frankie and me on Sunday morning? I had something I wanted to talk to them about.

As expected, they wanted to know what I wanted to talk to them about. I told them we'd wait until tomorrow to talk.

It was strange thinking; how could I have a tumor and cancer? I didn't feel sick. I didn't have any pain. What did the tumor on my lung have to do with my bladder bleeding anyway?

Sunday morning on the way to church and on the drive home Angela and Ritchie kept bugging me to tell them what I wanted to talk about.

I said, "You have to wait until we get home. I want to have the meeting when Frankie is there too so I can talk to all of you at one time."

I resisted the temptation of blurting it out right then and there. It was impossible to have the whole family there, for Joe and Greg lived out of town. Well, church was finally over and here we were in the driveway of our duplex.

We got out of the car and went into the house. I called Frankie and asked her to come over. Only a few minutes passed before she arrived, but it seemed like an eternity.

Finally, we were all sitting in the front room. Silence filled the air as we looked from one to the other.

The words I wanted to say had been right there on the tip of my tongue. But for the life of me I forgot what I was going to say. I'll never know why; I did end up just blurting it out.

I said, "I have cancer. I have a massive cancerous tumor in my lung. And I have cancer in my bladder." At this time, I didn't know I had it in my lymph nodes as well.

The room remained quiet for a minute and then everyone got up and was hugging me with tears flowing down their cheeks. At that very moment my thoughts flew to my granddaughter Megan. I wanted to have Megan come to the meeting but I knew she would be so distraught when she heard the news that I wouldn't be able to handle it.

She is sensitive and she loves me so much. I just couldn't face her with the information. I thought it would be better for her mom and dad to tell her. Megan is Angela and Ritchie's daughter.

We all began to cry again as they said, "Mom, we're here for you. Whatever it takes to fight this illness, we will do it with you."

Again, I was speechless. I had blurted out the problem and it left me weak and spent.

Later in the day Angela told Megan that I had cancer. She was hurt that we didn't include her in the family meeting, but she understood where I was coming from.

Megan called and through her tear-filled voice she told me she was sorry I was sick and that she would do whatever she could to help me.

True to her word, Megan would come visit me in the hospital and sit with me for hours. I got a kick out of her coming in and taking a nap in the recliner in the corner of the room. Having her visit me was comforting. She was such a blessing. She was sweet and kind and beautiful inside and out.

Megan and I were not just grandma and granddaughter, we were also best friends. We did so many things together. Our favorite, of course, was shopping. We loved spending hours on end in the clothing stores.

At this time, I'm no longer able to go shopping unless they have a cart I can ride. But it's okay. With all the medical expense, I don't have the money to spend anyway. I've learned to live with it and it doesn't bother me anymore.

True to her word, Angela started the ball to my recovery rolling by keeping the family informed of all that was going to happen, and what was going on from minute to minute. The changes came fast and furious.

Chapter 4
Getting Started

Having worked at Saint Elizabeth for six years, Angela knew a lot of the doctors and the staff that worked there.

She said. "Mom, I have the perfect radiologist and oncologist for you to see. I know them both. I've seen the oncologist in the halls and talked to her many times. Her name is Dr. Medathada."

I agreed and Angela made me an appointment.

After she scheduled a time with Dr. Medathada, she made me an appointment with the radiologist she recommended, Dr. Howell-Burke.

Dr. Howell-Burke is on staff at Saint Elizabeth. She informed me about the use of radiation they use to battle cancer.

Acting like I knew what she was talking about, I was dumbfounded, but agreed with all she told me.

I'm not sure what I was looking for when I walked into the oncologist office building. It was new and fresh-smelling.

The front office room was a relatively huge room with several office workers on one end, a fireplace, a TV and more rooms where they did the blood work and chemo treatments. There were quite a few office rooms as there were several other doctors in the same building.

The first time I saw Dr. Medathada walk into the room I was taken aback. I wasn't expecting her to be so young and beautiful. I liked her immediately.

She sat me down and explained the plan of action she was about to use to kill the cancer. She said, "While going through radiation treatments you need to have chemotherapy at the same time, along with bladder surgery."

I took this all in but I didn't know what I was in for, so once again, I said, "Okay then, I can do this."

She answered all my questions, but at the time, I didn't really know what questions to ask, because to tell the truth, I still wasn't aware of what cancer was or the way it attacks and destroys your being.

Oh yes, I'd heard about cancer all my life and knew people who had it and people who passed away from it. I never thought it could happen to me.

I kept telling myself that I was going to be one of the people who is going to defy the odds and not ever have to deal with all it entails.

I could tell Dr. Medathada was fond of Angela. It wasn't long before we became friends too. I actually looked forward to seeing her.

When it was all said and done, I did see a lot of her in the five years I was in her care. Although I grew to love her, I didn't love the things I had to go through in the lab whenever I went to her office.

Angela was ever vigilant, watching over me. She drove me to Dr. Medathada's office quite a bit the first two years of treatments. I went so often I began to know all the people that worked in the office.

We all got along well and soon I had a rapport with them, as they became a part of the support system I leaned on. However, I got a sinking feeling when I saw people I was acquainted with come into the office as I was waiting to see the doctor.

I'd be sitting there and I'd hear someone say, "Josie, hello, my friend, fancy meeting you here."

We'd hug and look at each other with the familiar look of 'I'm so sorry that you have cancer.' Both young and old in age, one worked in the grocery store I frequented and a few others were from the church I attended.

I am sorry to say that a certain friend of mine was at the oncologist's office for a second bout. She had been in remission but the cancer was back. She had been to Germany for treatments but she never made it; she passed away soon after we spoke in the oncologist's office building.

As I greeted people I knew, I began to recall a beautiful woman that was only forty years old that passed away from breast cancer. She was so brave, ministering and thinking of others right up to the last moment.

I never had a chance to tell her how much I loved and appreciated her. When I went to the hospital I was told she was too sick to see me. So, I am saying it now. I will remember her, always.

Each time I went to see Dr. Medathada, the nurses took me into a room where they took my blood. It wasn't long before I became very squeamish about having a needle stuck in my arm for any reason. So then, I began to cry whenever I see a needle coming at me. I hate to say it, but to this day, I still do.

After the first chemo treatment, anemia started to attack my body. I grew even weaker, so they scheduled me to take shots that burned my arm, and it took up to several minutes before they'd finally pull the needle out.

I was amazed when I learned the cost of those shots and other expenses.

Those particular shots cost $800.00 a shot. Medicare wouldn't pay anything unless the hemoglobin number was the number they designated that they would pay for.

Some cancer related pills cost $5,000.00 a pill. Another prescription I needed was $400.00 for six pills to combat the nausea that chemotherapy caused.

I don't think I could possibly have touched the bottom of the iceberg, so to speak. It was all so expensive.

I wasn't aware of the devastating expense that cancer treatments entail. It didn't dawn on me that having to pay twenty percent after Medicare was a great deal of money. Medicare was the only health insurance I had.

I assumed that some of the donations made to the cancer fund would help with some of the expenses. But that was not to be. The cancer office told me the donations go to research. Which is a good thing, but I think they should help people who couldn't afford medicine or whatever it took to get well.

Now maybe this isn't the way it occurs with some of the cancer cases, but it was the way it came to pass in my cancer experience. So, I can safely say that along with attacking one's body, cancer attacks one's billfold. It has taken me five years but I paid off most of the medical expenses I incurred during treatment. I am still working on several bills but hopefully they will be paid off soon.

The day I asked Frankie if she'd go to fill a prescription for me, she called me from the drug store to tell me it cost $400.00 for the six pills,

I said, "I can't afford that. Give the bottle of pills back to the druggist and forget it. Just come on home. Don't worry about it, we can talk about it when you get here."

When Frankie arrived at home I told her not to feel bad about not getting the pills. I would do all the little home remedy tricks I could think of to combat nausea.

I don't know for sure if this was a remedy at all, but I ate white soda crackers, blueberries, strawberries, raspberries, rice, salads and fruit smoothies.

I absolutely realize that everyone does not have the same reaction to medicine, pills, chemo, radiation and medical things as a whole. Nevertheless, I was still amazed when I found out that some people went through radiation and chemo and then they went to work right after they were done with the treatment. I contemplated why I couldn't react in the same way and that was when I had to accept that we all handle things differently. All I could do was the best I could. I got by in my own individual way.

I'd heard that eating fresh pineapple would help with anemia. So naturally I ate a lot of fresh pineapple. During this time, I began to study natural remedies and foods.

Two people that became two of my very best friends, Brad and Peg, encouraged me and gave me a lot of hints as to what to eat and drink. Peg had undergone cancer treatments so she kindly helped me with food ideas and encouragement. They are such good people. I love them so much.

Brad made me "Josie Cookies" to brighten my day. The cookie recipe that he named after me was his own special recipe made with apricots and coconut. Mmmmm, they were the best.

I ended up calling the oncologist office to tell them that I couldn't afford to fill the prescription. One of the nurses there found a few of the nausea pills that someone had donated to the clinic and she gave them to me.

Along with my home remedies, I used the pills sparingly and they lasted me for several weeks. Believe it or not, I struggled through the nausea with prayer, along with Angela and Frankie's tender loving care.

After this happened, somewhere along the way, Angela had me sign up for some help with the health and human services department so I could get help to pay for the medicine I needed. For sure, the only thing I knew about chemotherapy was that I would lose the hair on my head. I'm so stupid. Little did I realize that I'd lose every hair on my body including the hairs in my nose! It bothers me that my eyelashes didn't grow back as long as they were before chemo.

Losing my hair was such a small part of the after-effects of the chemo treatment, but it remained horrific to me. I couldn't stand to look at my bald head in the mirror. So, I avoided doing so at all costs.

It was around two-and-a-half years before I was able to get my hair done by my friend and beautician, Gail. She has been my beauty operator and consultant for twenty years and still is. She has been so supportive of me throughout all the years I've known her. When I first went back to see her was when my hair first came in, and it was very short and curly.

Losing my long red hair was only one of the traumatic experiences I encountered. It was one of my best features. I admit; I am kind of vain about my looks. In the long run it didn't help to lose every hair on my body, even in my nose.

Right before going to have my first chemo treatment I had my hair cut short by a hairdresser named Sandra. She was from Brazil. She had a sweet personality and always treated me so nice, so I tried to see her once in a while too.

It was after the first chemo treatment that my hair started coming out in clumps so I went back to see her and had her shave the rest of my hair off. Angela came with me and we all cried as my red locks fell to the floor.

Sometimes I wore a wig, but I didn't like to wear it. The wig felt heavy and itchy on my head. I wore stocking caps and caps that people made and donated to the clinic.

But mostly, I wore a red Nebraska stocking cap. I lived in sweats and pajamas. During this time, I used to tell everyone that I couldn't help it; I looked like a refugee.

My grandson Tobey, who was three at the time, started pulling my cap off, exposing my bald head and giving himself and all of us a good laugh.

Of course, wouldn't you know it, there was more. Along with losing my hair came the aches and pains, upset stomach, anemia, shots, blood transfusions, tingling legs and feet and other problems that cropped up during the treatment. I got so tired I didn't feel as if I could put one foot in front of the other. Sleep was my friend.

When the radiation and chemo treatments started you could have colored me confused because things didn't make sense anymore. Or I should say they made less sense than before.

I couldn't even get through the mail without feeling overwhelmed. There were several months where I just threw all the mail along with the bills in the trash. Needless to say, I smoked my last cigarette during this time.

When Frankie found out I was throwing the bills away she began to pay them. She didn't want me to deal with the consequences of having the utilities shut off, along with having bill collectors' threatening letters fill my mailbox.

As life rolled on, after the first chemo treatments I was advised to have a port put in. As expected, I had to have a different doctor for this procedure. His name was Dr. Cole. He put me into a twilight sleep in the surgery room and then inserted the port in above my right breast.

The port is where they administered chemo and gave me blood transfusions. The chemo was so strong that sometimes it pops your veins and they have to keep poking you with the needle to find a vein that could take the chemo chemical.

After my veins popped several times my oncologist told me that once I let the doctor put in the port, it would be easier to cope with the treatments.

Having become paranoid whenever I saw a needle coming at me, even having a port didn't help. I was still upset when they had to put needles in the port. Having the same nurse most of the time helped me cope.

She was sensitive to the way I felt so she always put something on the area to kind of deaden it so it didn't hurt as much while she was preparing me for the chemo treatment.

One day, while I was in the recliner watching the liquid chemo drip into my veins, I glanced up and noticed a lady sitting in the recliner chair across the room. The nurse was having a hard time getting her started. Her veins kept popping one after the other. They kept sticking and sticking her to find a vein that would work. Each time they did I felt so terrible for her I started to cry. The nurse called someone else in to help and they finally got the needle in her arm and got the medicine started. I was relieved for her.

There was so much that went on during this time, that even though I was going through a bad time, I felt there were others worse off than I was. I couldn't stand to see anyone suffer.

That freaking cancer monster reared its ugly head every chance it could.

I was fortunate to have someone like nurse Dave and nurse Angela who worked in the infusion section. They were caring and pleasant to everyone.

After my first bout with the chemo treatments, they put a small hospital bed in the back of the room with a curtain around it so I could lie down while going through the treatment. Usually when I was scheduled for the chemo treatments I'd be recouping from surgery and it was too hard for me to sit up in the recliners.

As the chemo dripped on I used to have to use the bathroom every ten minutes so they put a commode right next to the bed so I didn't have to wait for someone to take me to the restroom. That alone was taking most of their time and they had other patients to tend to. So, all in all they tried to make it as comfortable for me as they could.

I learned that chemo kills the good cells along with the bad cells. Sometimes I felt the cells going around and around, sloshing back and forth, growing back only to be killed again and again.

They took a lot of precautions administering the chemo. It was the cycle of life and death.

After the treatment was over, they told me not to let anyone use the toilet after me for three days. Golly, what was that all about? Well, I think it shows how toxic the chemo chemical is. With my vividly wild imagination, I had visions of someone using the toilet after me, and the toilet blowing up, 'Ka-boom!' Actually, I don't know what would have happened, but I don't think it is a good sign when they say take precautions.

I should have asked one of the nurses: What is the reason that people had to wait three days before using the toilet after me? I concluded that there were just too many other things to think of, and some of the questions I wanted to ask slipped my mind and went by the wayside. I just tried to remember and do all I was told.

Sometimes after a chemo treatment I had to have a blood transfusion. I'd never had one in my entire life so naturally, here I go again, acting brave on the outside, but inside, I was afraid. I didn't know what to expect. I didn't have a choice in the matter after I became anemic I had to have the blood transfusions to raise my hemoglobin.

One of the nurses joked around telling me the blood was from a sixteen-year-old and afterwards, I'd be able to run around the block.

I enjoyed having the medical staff put humor into situations because at times, I got so panicky over some of the procedures it was best to be as lighthearted as I could be. Which wasn't all the time, but there is a Bible scripture that says: "A merry heart does good, like medicine." It does seem that laughter has a healing effect, or who knows, maybe it just takes your mind off what is happening at the time.

For all my good intentions to trust God and deal bravely with each new treatment, fear crept into my being. Believe me, I'm not kidding when I say, I did a lot of praying during this time. When I felt my own strength ebbing slowly away, I believe that

God blew the breath of strength in me, willing me not to give up.

I'd say the "Our Father" prayer over and over again or sing hymns under my breath until whatever medical treatment they were doing with me was over.

It would have been easy to say, "The heck with this noise, I'm not doing anything else." I was always so self-sufficient. If I had something to say, it just flowed out of my mouth.

During this crucial time, I did take a stand for my well-being by refusing to use a doctor that was recommended. I went to see him once. I didn't care for him so I never went back. My oncologist then recommended a different doctor that I eventually hired to destroy the bladder cancer that was infecting my body. No small feat. I wanted to have someone I liked and trusted.

There was so much going on at one time, it made me woozy. I didn't have time to evaluate it in the same way I usually analyze everything.

Chemo treatments can also hurt your eyesight for a while as I found out the day I asked Angela if she would take me to the driver's license examining station. My license was about to expire and I didn't want that to happen even though I wasn't driving at the time. When I was asked to put my head in the machine they use to give the eye test, I tried to read the letters, but I couldn't make them out.

I guessed at a few letters and got them right but everything else was a blur. I told the lady I couldn't see well because of the chemo treatments. It was hard to believe that she passed me. I don't know if she felt sorry for me or didn't care if I drove and couldn't see to read the signs. But it was okay with me. To make matters worse, I had to have my picture taken with the long wig that I wore that day. Nevertheless, the picture turned out better than I thought it would.

I was bursting with pride at getting my license renewed. As I was patting myself on the back, I glanced around the room and there was a gentleman that passed his test and he couldn't speak English.

Suddenly I discerned what this could mean to drive on down the road with people who couldn't see or understand the rules of the road. Angela was shaking her head and repeating that she could hardly believe it.

The funny thing about this situation is that I'd had cataracts removed from both my eyes the year before I learned that I had cancer. I had gotten my eyesight back and didn't want to lose it again. Thank God, just a short while after I was done with chemo treatments my eyesight returned to what it had been before.

Along with the catch-22 of having to take radiation treatments that crept into my daily life came the unknown of what to expect from the radiation. Having radiation and chemo treatments at the same time threw me for a loop. The radiation treatments were Dr. Howell-Burke's expertise. The radiation activity she described sounded easy enough. Yet, after hearing her recommendation of forty-four straight days of radiation treatments to destroy the cancerous tumor, the number haunted me as I counted the days until they were over.

Right from the beginning the radiation equipment made me shudder. I had goose bumps everywhere. During the procedure I'd close my eyes so I wouldn't have to look at the red light that came on during treatment.

There were times as I was lying on the table on the pillow they made to fit my head, that I felt like I couldn't breathe, and it spooked me.

At a certain point the machine made a clicking noise. And that was when I began to be able to tell when the treatment was just about over.

I was uncomfortable lying on the table under the machine but I actually felt no pain while the radiation treatments were being administered.

I didn't realize radiation could cause damage that had such lasting, negative after-effects. I just thought of it as killing the cancerous tumor on my lung. I wasn't able to have surgery to remove the tumor. It had to be done with radiation and chemo.

One of the after-effects that troubled me after radiation treatments turned out to be fluid seeping into my lungs. The radiation as well caused a terrible rash on my chest that became infected and peeled the skin right off my body in the area where the radiation was killing the cancer. I ended up calling a druggist friend of mine that lived in another state to see what I could put on the skin infection. I'd been using an over-the-counter salve and it wasn't working. He recommended I use Silvadene. I called my doctor and asked if he would call in a prescription for the Silvadene salve. It worked like magic. It felt good to have my skin healing and going back to normal.

It was all agonizing, gross and scary. Having the strength zapped right out of me became a way of life. The treatments went on no matter how I was feeling.

Even after the bladder cancer surgery, I'd be wheeled into radiation or chemotherapy, or to an MRI or a CAT scan or a PET scan. Rain or shine, there I was under the radiation equipment.

I don't like to talk about all I've been through, but I feel the need to share some of it. I'm sure there are those who can relate to what I am saying? If not, I hope it will be beneficial to those who don't know.

There were so many days and nights I woke up sweating and then went into a chilling coldness. It was hard to get warm. I'd lie in bed feeling the blood coursing through my body. My heart pounded faster and faster, like a pendulum swinging back and forth.

Right after the radiation treatments stopped I was told I had to have my lungs drained because there was fluid flowing into them. The radiation had shrunk my lung.

This was hard to take. I was thinking, well, the radiation helped heal the cancer, but now what? I have to make more trips to the hospital for a course of action affiliated with the after-effects. I went for the treatment, naturally not knowing what to expect. I don't know how I could still have been so gullible, but I was. You'd think I would be aware that stuff happens and something could pop up that I wasn't expecting.

They put a needle in my back, shoving it up as far as they could to deaden the pain of sticking in a tube to drain the fluid into a bottle. I was shocked when I saw how much fluid they drained into the quart-sized bottles.

I wasn't fond of the first doctor so after going for three of those treatments I told my daughter that I refuse to go through that again.

It hurt badly when he was working on me. However, the second doctor that did this same procedure was gentle, working on me in such a way that it was not as excruciating.

When I went in for the third treatment, the hospital had scheduled me to be with the first doctor. I didn't care to see him. I wanted the second doctor that worked on me. For some reason I couldn't line him up again.

I gave in and went to see that same first doctor again. It was so unpleasant when he drained the fluid I couldn't catch my breath. I was gasping for air until Angela, who had been sitting there the entire time, asked him to stop.

When the fluid is drained it begins to hurt in the lung area and that's when you know it's done. I told the doctor it was beginning to hurt, but he just kept going and tried to drain more fluid. I can't figure out why he ignored my gasping and wheezing.

The doctors administering this particular procedure recommended that they could put a piece of equipment in my back so it would not be as painful to drain the fluid. And, it could be done at home. Otherwise, I could count on having to do the procedure at the hospital every three weeks for the rest of my life.

I thought it would be a good idea to get a second opinion so I took the advice of another doctor who worked in the oncologist office. She was seeing Dr. Medathada's patients while she was out of town. She recommended that I have the device put in my back by my right lung area that would drain the fluid out without the needle going up my back each time I had to have the liquid removed.

I said, "Okay then, if you think that is what I should do, then I'll have Angela set it up."

Okay then, I did it. I had the procedure done. It was uncomfortable and painful. I had a contraption hanging on my back now. The home health nurse came by several days a week to check on me and to show the family how to use the device in my back.

Right from the start, I felt like it wasn't working the way it should have. But then wanting to do what was best I kept trying to go along with the agenda. Every time the health nurse put the tube in the contraption, there was very little fluid that came out. It was building up in my lung and making me feel even more uncomfortable. After several weeks, I couldn't stand it any longer. It was so hard to breathe I went crying to Dr. Medathada, who at this time was back in town.

When I saw her walking up the hall toward her office, I ran up to her and asked to have it removed. I was crying and panicky. She put her arms around me and said, "Not to worry, we'll take care of this." She immediately sent me to the hospital where they removed the apparatus that had been stabbing me in the back. Evidently it had been resting on a nerve.

Once more, Angela took the bull by the horns and made the arrangements at the hospital. Whoa-de-oh-do, here I go again. It didn't take long to have the device removed. It was painless and felt so good to have the apparatus removed.

After they had removed the apparatus, a kindly doctor came in to the hospital room to talk to me. He described a surgery procedure that could help so I wouldn't have to go through draining my lungs for life. He said, "Think about it and let me know. We can arrange to have it done right away."

Although I had some complications along the way, I was still agreeable to do whatever it took to feel better. But somewhere along the way, as I became more and more skeptical, fear continually worked its way into my daily routine. Sometimes, I used to question if God ever got tired of hearing me cry out to him so many times to give me power to endure.

I couldn't get over some of the things I thought of when overcoming each new obstacle in my quest to be a cancer survivor/warrior.

Of all things I'd think of my sister, Antoinette, saying, "I think God has a sense of humor and that is why he keeps me around so he can have a few more laughs."

I contemplated her words thinking, yes, that has to be for me too. I'm good for a few laughs.

All kidding aside, I don't know how, and I don't know why things happen the way they do. I don't have the answers. Why one person gets healed and the other doesn't. But still, I firmly believe that there is an Almighty, awesome God of the universe, and that God is the great healer. I think miraculous miracles and healings are meant for today as well as they were meant for those in biblical times.

On the other hand, I also believe God uses doctors, medicine and medical procedures, blessing us with good health care. How fortunate we are to live in a day and age with so much technology, curing ailments and diseases that there was no cure for years ago.

I grew up in an era when there was no cure or vaccine. Young children and adults were afflicted with, to name a few, polio, small pox, and rheumatic fever. A home could be quarantined for any kind of disease, including measles, mumps, and chicken pox.

Even though I don't understand the how and the why, I am thankful to God for the men and women who have the talent and ability to work with medicine and healing, coming up with a cure for devastating diseases. All the same, I did understand one thing for sure, and that was the agenda that one has to go through before surgery. The preparations are line upon line.

I disliked having to take the medicine they put in my body intravenously. I detested taking pills. Even having to take an aspirin would send me into a tizzy.

Watching the movie "As Good As It Gets," I could relate to the movie star, Jack Nicholson, when he said, "I hate pills. I'm using the word hate." I said aloud, "Thanks, for that analogy Jack, which is exactly the way I feel."

I was always nervous about taking pills. When my husband was alive, I never took a pill unless he was home to watch me swallow it. I'd have him stay with me until I made sure I wasn't going to have an allergic reaction.

My doctor never knew all the times I flushed pills down the toilet so I wouldn't have to take them. I knew it was a terrible, wasteful thing to do but I couldn't help myself. The phobia just took over. No matter how many times I told everyone, no one seemed to take seriously just how much I hated taking pills. Besides the fact that part of me was afraid to take them. When

I was not in the hospital, I'd ask someone in the family to stay with me until I swallowed the pills.

In my younger years I had a bad allergic reaction to penicillin. I broke out in hives and everything went black. I was rushed to a hospital where they gave me a shot to counteract it. The doctor told me that I had a reaction to the drug and that I might die if I ever took penicillin again.

Well, so much for penicillin or any other medicine. Those words made a cynic out of me. Especially when I learned that I couldn't even take antibiotics that were related to penicillin. Two of the medicines I can't take are Ancef and Levaquin, which are both related to penicillin. I had an allergic reaction to both of them while I was in the hospital. Now whenever I am given an antibiotic prescription I call the druggist and ask if it is a penicillin product. I didn't ever want to take another pill again. But naturally, at this point in my life, I was not going to be that lucky.

Being afraid and leery to take drugs didn't just happen overnight and it wasn't just because I had a reaction. It happened over the years as other members of my family had an allergic reaction to certain medicines.

I can't remember all the times my children were allergic to certain things, but I still remember a few.

For instance, there was the time that Frankie had an allergic reaction to a pill called Compazine that she took for nausea. She was deforming right before our very eyes. Her body went limp, her head was bent sideways and her hand and arm were twisted. We had to rush her to the hospital. The doctor gave her a shot to counteract it. To this day I say I am allergic to that particular medicine.

To make matters worse, one day I got a telephone call telling me my son, Joe, had a terrible reaction to a pill called Topamax. It was prescribed to him for a headache. He took the pill for seven days and then he had a reaction. He went out like a light. His daughter, Drenda, walked in the room and found him lying on the floor. He was rushed to the hospital in Tennessee. He had lost his sight. His eyes looked gray and red. He was one sick boy. While in the hospital, the doctor did laser surgery. It took a while but his eyesight returned. He was so thankful to be able to see again, he didn't blame anyone or want retribution. He gave God glory and honor for his healing.

Here I go again, I now feared this particular pill and so what do I do, I list it as one of my allergies too. Angela laughs at me for listing this one. I felt that if my children were allergic, then so was I.

Now, it doesn't mean that someone taking the medicine I talk about would have the same reaction. I am not an authority on the subject. The medicine may do some good to others who are not allergic. The situations I described happened and I am simply sharing them. Not to be double-minded, I felt it was essential to list the names of the medicines.

It feels good to share this information for I'm aware that there are so many people out there that have had bad reaction experiences that can relate to whatever experience they have had with medicine that caused a reaction. Nevertheless, I'm thinking sometimes it is just not anyone's fault that the wrong medicine was prescribed. We don't really know what anyone is allergic to until they try it.

Once again, though, I have to admit, I am suspicious when it comes to taking any kind of medicine

.

Chapter 5
Life's a Whirlwind

Angela continued to take the bull by the horns. She unceasingly scheduled appointments with the doctors and hospital and she literally carried me in the palm of her hand.

The name Angela means angel, and that is exactly what she is. She is an angel walking on the face of the earth. Each time she explained the schedule of things to come, little did I know all it entailed or that before it was all said and done, I had to see more than half a dozen different doctors.

That's when the whirlwind really began.

One day I had three doctor appointments and one hospital test. By the time we got to the last appointment we were totally pooped out.

I turned to Angela and said, "After all we've been through today, this doctor better be good-looking." We laughed and talked a bit more. Then guess what Angela did when we were finally called to go into the doctor's office? She told him what I said about having a good-looking doctor. To say the least, I was embarrassed. By the way, he was good-looking, handsome and gorgeous.

The next day we went back to the oncologist where the tiny, beautiful lady from India, Dr. Medathada, informed me that without treatment I had six months to a year to live.

After listening very carefully I said, "Okay then, I guess I don't have much of a choice. I think I'm ready to do whatever it takes."

I could tell right off the bat that she was very intelligent and knew her business. That gave me some confidence and made me feel a little more at ease.

Dr. Medathada told me that I would need a pulmonologist. Dr. Miller, being one of the best, was recommended for this job. I continued to go from one appointment to the other. None of the news was good.

Although this was at the beginning stage of treatments, I wonder, with all the bad news, how come I felt okay? I was discouraged and depressed but at this particular time, I wasn't sick or hurting anywhere. Well, not yet anyway.

Yet again, I spoke too soon. This was all about to change and those thoughts never plagued me again.

The next test I had to go for was a PET scan. This was added to my list of one of my least favorite tests.

The nurse inserts a needle in your arm, and that injects radioisotopes that go into your vein. Then she leaves you in a room by yourself for forty-five minutes to an hour, where she watches you on a screen in another room. You have to be perfectly still and not move an inch.

As I sat in the room, my mind was racing. I was silently praying and singing hymns the whole time.

I can't deny that I was also thinking about the highly toxic radioisotopes coursing through my veins.

Having an aversion to being left alone in a small closed-in room, I was relieved when the nurse opened the door. I clapped my hands and said, "I'm so glad to see you. Calgon, take me away from all this!"

She smiled and wheeled me to another room where they put me into a circular tube for twenty-five minutes. It was so small my arms had to be inserted in bandage type sheeting that holds them down by your side. Being claustrophobic, it was not easy for me to be inside the small space. Once again in my brain, I silently prayed and sang to myself.

It wasn't that long until she said, "Okay, you're done. That wasn't so bad, was it?"

"Yes, it was, but thanks for being done and for caring about me," I replied.

The nurse said, "I'm going to put you back in the wheelchair. We are on our way to do an MRI on your brain now."

I made a face and said, "Do I have to? I'm so tired I just want to go home."

"I'm sorry, but your doctor ordered the test," she replied. I said, "Okay then, lead the way."

She led the way to another part of the hospital. By this time, I was panicking inside. Everything looked so uninviting in the room where they wheeled the patients. Even the reception area seemed drab.

The nurse said, "I am leaving you here for now. When they are done, someone will take you to your daughter in the waiting room."

I thanked her and sat quietly until one of the male nurses came over and wheeled me into the testing room.

I was not ready for what was about to happen. They put me in the circular cylinder and then a hammering sound started pounding. After fifteen minutes they pulled me to the opening of the tube to check on me. As I emerged to the front of the tube, I grabbed the nurse and cried, "Please, don't make me do any more."

She said, "Not to worry my dear, I believe we have enough data. You don't have to do anymore. Let's get you dressed and I'll take you to the waiting room. It's all right now, don't cry. You did a real good job."

Through tear-swollen eyes I said, "Thank you. I'm sorry if I am acting like a baby. I'm just so tired."

"Don't worry about it. You did just fine," she said.

I got dressed and she wheeled me into the waiting room. Angela saw me coming and she jumped up and rushed to my side. I tried to act upbeat but as she was wheeling me out to the car, tears gushed from my eyes. She started to cry and we walked down the hospital hallway that way.

Angela said, "Mom, I can't stop crying until you do."

I simply said, "Okay."

It took me about ten minutes but at last the tears subsided. And once again we were on our way home.

We stopped at McDonald's for a sandwich and a cup of coffee. Yep, once more, they messed up our order and it was good for the day's laughter.

We had started a ritual of going to McDonald's every day that we were out and about, which seemed to be every day. I don't know why we never went anywhere else. We'd see the yellow arch and we'd just naturally pull in and give them our order. Not meaning to get on the establishment, but it seemed that each time we went through the drive-thru, they messed up our order. We began to joke about it. We made bets on what they would mess up next.

The next day, Frankie took me to the urologist office of Dr. Wiltfong. I detested the procedure he had to use to check my bladder. It consisted of inserting a tube with a camera on the end into my urethra up into my bladder. When he reached the destination, it showed that my bladder was filled with cancer. The doctor said, "Go ahead and look at the screen if you want to."

"I don't know if I want to," I said.

I was squeamish at first, but then I peeked at the screen that was on the side of the room right near the table, within the doctor's best sight.

I'll never forget the way it looked. My bladder was a grayish white color. The cancer looked like whitish looking algae grass floating back and forth, like the algae grass floating at the bottom of the ocean.

It felt so strange to be looking into the face of cancer. It looked beautiful, and it looked ugly at the same time. It was weird to describe what I was seeing. It was what it was, though, scary and destructive. Finally, the examination was over.

He pulled out the tube with the camera on the end of it. I breathed a sigh of relief.

Dr. Wiltfong said, "You are going to need laser surgery to remove the cancer."

Blinking back the tears, all I could say was, "Is this going to hurt?"

The doctor looked at me with compassion and said, "Very little."

I liked Dr. Wiltfong right from the start. Little did I know the laser treatment would be the easiest procedure I would go through in the next two years!

I left his office feeling dizzy and light headed. I was as gray as the clouds in the sky overhead. I caught Frankie looking at me, and she looked so miserable. Once more, here I go again, needing to act like I was a valiant soldier when all the time my insides were shaking. I speculated; does it ever end?

The answer that came to me on that specific question was, maybe and maybe not. Confusion is lurking in the background, ever ready to pounce on me. I wave my arms in the air trying get rid of it.

But on the whole, believe it or not, I began to think that I was better off not knowing exactly what to expect when the doctors told me what I had to do.

There was one thing I could do and that was to trust fully in God and not waver in my faith, and believe I was going to win the rampant war that was intensely raging on with no letup in sight. I might lose a battle here and there but I was determined to win the war against the uninvited cancer enemy that was squeezing its way into my territory.

The next morning, I got a call from the urologist's office with the day and time I was scheduled to have bladder surgery and the instructions I had to follow.

The arrangements were made, so here I was getting ready to go again. It was five thirty a.m. when I checked into the hospital for bladder surgery.

Chapter 6
Surgery

The day arrived, and Angela drove me the hospital where we met Frankie. They both came into the small cubicle room where the nurse was putting in an IV, checking my vital signs and trying to make me feel less anxious.

As my daughters watched over me, I could see the look of fear in their eyes. This particular morning, trying to be strong for my children was taking its toll. I just didn't have the strength to keep it up as fear of the unknown suddenly overtook me. I felt frightened.

I was crying when Dr. Jirovec walked into the area they put me in before surgery. I was so glad to see his sympathetic face. Although he wasn't doing the surgery, he wanted to be there to support me.

I looked at his kind eyes and thought about what a wonderful doctor he was. He wasn't just wonderful; he was a sweet and caring human being. Just knowing he was there made me feel a little calmer. I can't help it. I just can't stop saying what a great guy he is.

While he was talking, the nurse came in the tiny cubicle. She said, "It's time to take you into surgery," and she wheeled me away."

I glanced back at Dr. Jirovec, and my two daughters who were standing there with weeping eyes. Everything flashed before me as the nurse briskly whisked me down the hall. She took me into a room and began to start another IV. Immediately after liquid dripped into my vein I began to have an allergic reaction. I broke out in hives. My head and body began to itch and my face started to swell up. They hurried me into the operating room and put me out.

The next thing I knew I was waking up in the recovery room. Naturally I asked the nurse about what drug was used in the IV. This is when I found out that I was allergic to yet another antibiotic called, Levaquin.

The surgeon, Dr. Wiltfong, went into the waiting room to talk to my family and let them know I came through the surgery okay. He soon came into the intensive care room and told me I would be taken to my room in just a few minutes.

Dr. Wiltfong is another of my favorite doctors. He had a bedside manner that I could live with. He helped to save my life by destroying the fatal cancer lurking in my bladder. I was up and at them, shortly after surgery.

I had to have a doctor that showed kindness. I just couldn't get myself to compromise when it came to having a doctor take care of me who didn't act with compassion. It was okay if they were all business but to act like I was a number is a no-no with me.

I wasn't in the room long before my daughters came in to see me. I was still groggy but it was a relief to know it was over. I told them they should go home and rest awhile. I was out of it and didn't feel like talking just yet. I just wanted to sleep. They left and came back at suppertime.

By that time, I was alert and we all tried to be in good humor. They brought candy and flowers and tried to make me feel special. Time went fast and soon they went home again.

A few hours after surgery, a nurse came in and said, "Let's get you up and try to walk in the hall a little."

I said, "You've got to be kidding."

She said, "No ma'am. I'm not kidding. We are going for a stroll."

I tried to make light of it and said to the nurse, "Okay then, I'll race you to the window at the end of the hall."

I moved pretty slow but felt like it was an accomplishment to just get out of bed. After we walked a little way up the hall, the nurse was sensitive enough to know I did the best I could so she steered me back to my room.

Getting into bed was a chore in itself. I am short and the bed seemed a mile high off the floor. She went and got me a step stool. Ah, that was much easier; I could actually get into bed without a struggle.

From then on, no matter how many times I went into the hospital, they put a step stool in my room. They kept it by my bed so I could get in and out without having to call someone to help me.

Back snug in my bed, I had an IV, drainage tubes and a catheter. To say I was uncomfortable was putting it mildly. It is hard to believe, but sometime during the night I woke up and actually asked the nurse if I could go for another walk down the hall. She smiled and said, "Oh yes, "It is so good to get up and move as much as you can after surgery."

She helped me up and walked down the hall with me. This time I went a little further.

When I got back to the room I asked if I could sit in the reclining chair. She said I could and she helped me get situated. I went in and out of sleep and before I knew it, Dr, Jirovec was there.

He said, "It is good to see you sitting up."

I replied, "I was restless last night. It was hard to sleep so I had the nurse take me for a walk."

"You did really well and will probably be going home tomorrow," he said.

I quickly replied, "That's fine with me. I'm ready to go home."

"Dr. Wiltfong will be in to see you soon. I'll see you later," he said. With that he walked out of the room.

"Thanks for stopping by Doc; see you," I remarked.

It was only a matter of minutes before Dr. Wiltfong arrived. He confirmed that I was doing good and that I would be in the hospital just one more day and then I could go home.

The bladder surgery took place during the time I was still having radiation and chemo treatment. Being scheduled for a radiation treatment shortly after bladder surgery, in came the person from radiology to load me up.

I began to know most of the people that worked in the different departments in the hospital, so when they came to get me in a wheelchair we began to joke around. They were vibrant young men and women that made you feel at ease.

I didn't feel like running around the block or anything, but I was trying hard to do what I was told.

Even though radiation makes you really tired and I was still weak from surgery, we got through the procedure. Soon I was on my way back to my room.

I was ready to go to sleep, but my daughter Angela was in the room waiting for me with flowers in her hand and a smile on her face.

I was so fortunate. It was comforting to have a relative working in the hospital. That way she could check on me at all times. Some of the people that worked with her sent me cards and flowers and came by to see me, along with the nuns and clergy.

Everyone I met at Saint Elizabeth Catholic hospital was so nice. They told me how much they loved Angela. The nuns made me a prayer shawl. I wasn't sure what that was but they explained to me that they prayed over each stitch they put in the shawl. The first morning I was scheduled to have a radiation treatment, the nuns and some of the staff gathered around me in the waiting room and each of them prayed for me. I liked the prayers and knowing that God and Jesus are welcomed guests in the hospital.

During and after radiation and chemo treatments started I was scheduled for several different surgery procedures. I tried to maintain a healthy attitude, but I worried about what was next. It was getting to me when some medical procedures produced an after-effect.

It was all happening way too fast.

Chapter 7
Little Did I Know

After my lungs filled up with fluid again, I decided to go through with the surgery the doctor had recommended after I had the device taken out of my back. I couldn't stand the thought of having my lungs drained every three weeks.

He further explained that during the procedure they would put some kind of material into my lungs that hardens so fluid can't get in there. They'd have to move my rib some and I would be hooked up to an IV with tubes connected to the lung area that would not be removed until a few days after surgery.

After I was put through the course of action getting ready for another surgery, once again, I consoled my children. It was heartbreaking to see the look in their eyes whenever they saw me lying on a bed about to be wheeled into the surgery area. Geez, wouldn't you know it, after they hooked me up and shoved in all the needles, here I was allergic to another antibiotic called Ancef. The symptoms that it provoked were considered a small problem, and I was rushed into the surgery room where everything went black.

This time, I was really out of it. When I woke up, I was groggy and hooked up to morphine pain medication where you can press a button when the pain gets to be too harsh, and it administers more.

Of all things, I worried about not knowing when to press the button if the pain got too horrific, but I soon learned that was the least of my worries.

They wheeled me back into the room. I can't remember how long it was before I had to call the nurse and gasp out that I couldn't breathe. I was making a funny noise trying to get air into my lungs but it wasn't happening. They rushed me into another part of the hospital and hooked me up to a ventilator.

The hospital called my children. They told my girls to come back to the hospital right away. They didn't know if I would make it through the night.

The children drove back to the hospital. In the haze of pain and medicine and shaking on the ventilator, I could see them standing there crying. Holding on to each other, staring at me while I was on the machine, doing the shake, rattle, and roll dance. I didn't want them to see me this way. I started praying, asking God to make them to go home and get some rest. It was breaking my heart to see how distressed they were. They didn't know what to do so, Angela called Ritchie. He told them to go home and get some sleep. I don't know how much time passed before they finally left the room and went home.

I was hurting, miserable and sick. But I do remember needing to press the nurse's call button to come help me. The same nurse came into the room each time and when she did, she was ill-mannered and rude.

During the course of the night, I felt like I was in a limbo land. I went in and out of the mist. The machine was helping me to breathe.

Nevertheless, I didn't sleep soundly the entire night. I was in a daze, in a haze. It was like I was in a fog where you can't see the light at the end of the tunnel. It was just dim and cloudy. I could barely make anything out.

However, going through all that with my pain-wracked body shaking through the night to keep me alive, I was aware that the nurse on duty was mistreating me. In the two years I was in and out of the hospital that was the only nurse that acted rude and uncaring. It was not the best time to have to put up with a nurse who didn't care about me and she let me know she didn't. I couldn't believe that this could be happening when I was in the worst kind of pain and fighting for my life hooked up to the ventilator.

The discourteous nurse may have thought it was a long night for her, but it was a very long night for me too. She made no bones about letting me know she was upset with me. She was actually disturbed because she thought I pressed the call button way too often for someone to come into the room to tend to me. She kept telling me she had other patients.

I was so out of it. The doctors were trying to keep me alive on the ventilator and here I was, not making her day by asking for help. She wasn't aware of anything but herself.

I couldn't believe how weak I was. I wanted to say to her, what is wrong with you? I couldn't tell her she wasn't making my night very pleasant either, but I was in no shape to fight with the help. I wasn't even able to talk yet.

Somehow the night passed. Early the next morning Angela called the hospital to ask about my progress. After talking to this particular nurse, she knew something was amiss and she came running to the hospital. The nurse that was irritated with me ran up to her and said, "We have to talk about your mom. She keeps turning the call light on and we have other patients to tend to besides her."

Angela, who would normally have let her have, this time just smiled and walked on into my room. Although it ticked her off, her concern was not with the nasty nurse, it was with me.

We were going to turn her in and write her up but we didn't. I thought we should have reported it so she couldn't treat someone else the way she treated me. But then again, maybe sometimes it is good to just walk away from the insanity. I wasn't sure this was one of those times, but at the moment I was too sick to sort it out. Besides, knowing Angela, she might have turned her in without telling me.

Then, like a miracle, the next morning one of the doctors came in and took me off the ventilator. The doctor said, "Josie, you don't need to be on the ventilator anymore, you're breathing on your own now. You can go back down to the fifth floor."

"Thank you, doctor. You've made me a happy camper," I remarked.

If I could have jumped for joy, I would have. Oh boy, the day was starting out just great. Although I was still in much pain, hooked up to tubes and a catheter, I was anticipating the move to another floor where the staff treated me with tender loving care.

Well, now, I can write it. At the time I could hardly talk and was too sick to confront her, but if she could have read my thoughts it would have been something like this, "I'm leaving this floor Miss Nasty Nurse. Go back to school for some lessons on bedside manners."

Thank God! I was glad I would soon be out of her clutches. To this day though, I can't believe that even when I felt better, I let her off the hook.

Later that evening, some of the aides came and got me ready to take me to another floor. I was hurting and tired. I just couldn't get back into the wheelchair again, so they let me stay in bed. While they were wheeling me out of the room we passed by the nurse's station where "Nurse Ratched" was standing. I caught her eyes as she looked at me with a malicious-looking grin on her face and she waved at me.

It was then and there that I nicknamed her "Nurse Ratched" after the nurse in the movie, 'One Flew Over The Cuckoo's Nest.'

I am a movie buff. The dialogue in movies pops into my head about certain situations and sometimes at the weirdest times. I remember looking at her and thinking, what kind of person is that? I don't know and I guess it is not up to me to know. She is who she is. I am who I am. I had bigger things on my mind. They wheeled the bed onto the elevator and took me down to the fifth floor where they gently helped me into another bed.

After I was situated in the room, Angela and Frankie came in along with my son Joe, who flew in from Tennessee. I was so happy to see him. He was holding a big stuffed bunny that he bought for me in the gift shop. I kept it on my bed the rest of the time I was in the hospital. I still keep it on my bed at home. He brought his laptop with him so he could stay with me during the day and work on his computer at the same time. He owned his own business and needed to keep in touch with it.

The next day my son, Greg, came up from Kansas. So now all my children were by my bedside. I love my children so much. They make my world go around.

Dr. Medathada came into the room while the children were hovering around me. I introduced them to her. They were impressed with the way she comforted and informed me of my progress.

That evening, Joe was asking me questions and my answers were not coherent. He asked me where I was. I said I was in another state other than the one I was in. Then he asked my name and I didn't know it. He realized something was wrong, so he called the nurse into the room. The nurse said I was getting way too much pain medication, and she adjusted the valve.

I felt bad that I was so out of it I could barely hold a conversation with anyone. I couldn't even pick up a fork to eat dinner. Just then, Greg, Angela and Megan walked into the room. Greg fussed over me for a while, being ever so glad to see me. He didn't get to see his family very often, so he was happy to be with us, even if it was in a hospital.

My son in-law Richard, who is more like a son to me, used to come and have supper with me. He wasn't fond of being in hospitals, so I thought of it as a special time that I hold dear in my heart. Sometimes I slept through his visits but just having him in the room was comforting.

The children didn't often have much of a chance to all be together at one time. Although the circumstances were bad, I was glad they were all together enjoying one another's company.

During the time they were here, the staff came into the room to meet them. They kidded back and forth, and as miserable as I felt, it was a fun time to have all my children in one place. Joe stayed a few days and then had to go back to Tennessee. I hated to see him go, but understood his job and family needed him. I was thankful that he came to be with me. Greg left the same day and things quieted down again.

The next day was Frankie's birthday. Angela and my granddaughter Megan came to visit and we celebrated it in my hospital room. Frankie brought in a cake and pizza. We all sang happy birthday to her. We shared the goodies with a nurse who got a kick out of our celebration.

I had Angela pick me up a gift for Frankie and it was a real party. I couldn't let her birthday go by just because I was in the hospital.

It wasn't long after surgery that the medical team thought I should go to a rehabilitation center. I was released a week later. They took me in a van to the place where I was scheduled to do rehabilitation.

I can't put my finger on any one thing that turned me against staying at the place they drove me to.

The personnel running the place seemed nice enough. They were probably helping a lot of people in need. There were sure a lot of employees and patients scurrying around. My attitude could possibly have been a case of 'it's not you, it's me' philosophy.

Maybe it was taking in the whole scene of what was happening all around me as they wheeled me through the front door. There were old people with blank expressions on their faces, lined up sitting in wheelchairs right near the door by the front desk. Everywhere I looked, there seemed to be working staff and patients wandering around.

I can't explain why I was letting my first impression guide my thinking, but it was.

They wheeled me down the hall and into a tiny space with another person sharing the room. There was a radio blaring in the next room and out in the hallway there were young people scurrying around.

When I asked for a private room I was told that I couldn't have one because they didn't have one available. And then, one of the employees told me that I was on Medicare and they wouldn't pay for a private room. I told the person in charge that I didn't want to stay there. By this time, I wanted to go home in the worst way.

It wasn't long before someone came in and told me I could have a private room, but by then I knew for certain that I didn't want to be there. I asked, "What changed to warrant me a private room?"

They didn't answer. Several attendants came into the room and put me in another wheelchair and zoomed me down the corridor into a private room.

It was a nice room with a view of the street, trees and flowers, but something about the whole thing turned me off. They were all very nice, but something about the place in itself and the attitudes there turned me off.

I asked to use the telephone and I was told that it didn't work because I had to have it turned on in my name. However, someone did finally come in the room and connected it for me so I could make a call to my daughter.

They didn't seem to be too happy that I wanted to leave. That seemed a bit strange to me. Besides, I wasn't interested in what they thought of me. I simply wanted to get out of there and go home as fast as I could.

I called Frankie to come pick me up. Then I called a friend and asked her to call and tell Angela that I was coming home. There was a twenty-four-hour oxygen tank in the front room because I couldn't get down stairs to my apartment. I slept on Angela's sofa for several days.

The tubing was fifty feet long and was curled up in the middle of the floor. Everyone had to watch where he or she walked. Angela and Richard supported my decision, but I wasn't sure if they were happy that I didn't stay for more treatment. I think they were reluctant for they thought I needed the structured environment of a rehabilitation facility.

Well, too late now. I'm home and pleased to be here.

I needed to have some control over my life. Wanting to cooperate with everyone, it seemed as if I was doing what everyone else wanted me to do. I wasn't a puppet on a string; I still had a mind. I wanted to use it to know what was best for me.

We made arrangements for the home health nurse to come to the house to help me. She arranged for a bath lady and a physical therapist to assist me.

I only used the bath lady once. I was a bit sheepish about having someone in the bathroom with me while I stripped down to my birthday suit.

She handed me the washcloth and said, "Here, wash your girls." I'm sure that her little ditty was meant to be funny, but little did she know that it was going to be the last time I would need her assistance.

One thing I try to be is hip and cool, but way down deep I am so old-fashioned, one would not believe that of me.

But then again, who really knows exactly what is in one's heart? I live in a world that I don't know anymore. But I have to keep on top of what is important to me. My independent spirit took another stand. I told the bath lady that she didn't have to come back, for I was able to take care of my grooming needs all by myself. I guess I am from the old school of not wanting anyone to view me in the bathtub in my birthday suit.

Chapter 8
Circumstances

Each time I was hospitalized I had to be on oxygen. This specific time when I was discharged from the hospital, it was with the understanding that I was to be on oxygen twenty-four hours a day.

That bothered me immensely. I felt uncomfortable going to bed with the tubes in my nose and the hum of the oxygen machine, along with walking around with fifty feet of tubing dragging behind me. I had enough tubing so that I could walk to the kitchen and back to my bedroom.

During the course of this time, I considered that having to be on oxygen all the time was a pain in the behind. Someone had to carry the portable oxygen tank up the stairs and out to the car with me attached to it. It was a small cylinder, but even that was way too heavy for me to pick up. I had to use a walker and drag around the portable oxygen tank at the same time.

We kept a large oxygen tank in the garage to fill the portable tank. I wanted to get off it in the worst way. I didn't tell anyone that I was beginning to wean myself off the oxygen. Each night I started to take the tube out of my nose for a period of time. Just a few minutes at first, then an hour, then two hours until I got up to the point where I kept it off all night long.

When I decided to tell the health nurse that I didn't need to be on oxygen anymore, she said that I had to be tested before she would okay taking me off of it.

She brought me an apparatus to hook up to that would take my oxygen level all through the night without my taking the oxygen. Voila, the next morning my oxygen level was ninety and above all through the night. It is considered low if it is below ninety.

Then I had to go to see Dr. Miller, my pulmonary doctor. They tested me by having me walk around and taking my oxygen level while I walked. It was okay during exercise, and so she said I didn't have to be on it anymore.

Hooray, I did it. I am oxygen-free. It was like graduating from one level to another.

Angela told me it was practically unheard of to be taken off of oxygen. Most people who had what I have are on it for life. I'm not recommending what I did for everyone. If someone wants to try this, they should check with their doctor first before doing what I did.

I regarded being taken off of oxygen as just one of the miracles that took place during this time. After it was all was said and done, I started to tell everyone that I was a walking medical miracle.

I truly did believe God was healing me even though I had a long way to go yet. I was thankful to God for all his love and mercy.

Even though more setbacks and surgery were coming my way, my heart was set on being off medicine and taking care of myself. After I was taken off the oxygen, each time I was hospitalized I got nervous when they hooked me up to it again.

When I got sick my oxygen level went back down to a dangerous level. I was worried that the doctor would keep me on it when I was released from the hospital. But as it turned out, when the IV medication took effect and I started to feel better, my oxygen level would start to even out and stay at a safe level. I was trying to cut down on the many trips I had to make to the hospital and to doctor's appointments. I had my own agenda.

Little by little I made strides toward my goal. I had setbacks I had to deal with, but they were soon behind me.

The radiation and chemo did what they were supposed to do. They killed the cancer cells.

Now I was battling the after-effects. I was learning to live with pain in my right side, under my breast along my side up to the middle of my back. It was there all the time. I could live and function and do a few things with the pain during the day, but come nighttime the pain seemed to step up, so I took a hydrocodone pain pill. I didn't want to take pain pills all day long, so I kept it down by merely taking one pill in the evening only. On the whole, I tried to be as self-sufficient as I could be and do things for myself.

After I was through with the radiation and chemotherapy treatments and surgeries, I became very ill. I couldn't stop coughing. I had to go through more CAT scans and x-rays.

The scans and the x- rays continued to show the damage in my right lung and some spots, but they showed that the cancer cells were gone - killed dead by the poisons.

That should have been cause for celebration. And it was, but I was way too sick to grasp the full meaning.

The latest test showed that I had pneumonia.

With my history of lung problems, catching pneumonia was dangerous and it worried the doctors. I ended up in the hospital for nine days.

By this time, after numerous IVs, I was tired of having my hand punctured again and again. It made me fearful when the IV machine would buzz. Sometimes it meant that the medicine wasn't coming through right, or the bag had to be changed. Why this occurrence disturbed me I'll never know. It just did.

Because I was allergic to so many antibiotics, the doctors thought steroids should be used to help combat the pneumonia. Having diabetes, the steroids in turn put my blood sugar level at an all- time high. My blood sugar level continued to climb so high that along with the Januvia pill I took for diabetes, I had to have four to five insulin shots a day to counteract the effect of the steroids on my blood sugar level.

My family and friends came to see me as much as they could. I was so sick it was hard to visit for long periods of time. It troubled me when I didn't recognize Denise, one of my very best friends for twenty-five years, when she walked into my hospital room.

It was hard to talk on the telephone. I'd say hello and that was about as far as I got. Yet my sister, Mary, and my brother, Mike, called me long distance every night to check up on me. It meant a lot to me that my brother and sister called me every day from the time they heard I had cancer.

Mike had undergone some excruciating cancer treatments. I could not imagine going through what he had to go through in his bout with cancer. Little did he know that it was too late; the cancer had traveled too far.

Angela called my sister Skeets the night I was on the ventilator. She said, "Skeets, I thought I should call and tell you that the hospital staff informed me that they didn't know if Mom is going to make it through the night. This is the prognosis that was told to me this evening, so I thought I should call and tell you what was going on."

After I finally made it back to my room, my sister and brother Mike started the telephone vigil. Skeets has called me every day since then, to this day. I love talking to her. We find so much to talk about.

Then the news came that Mike had passed away. It upset me so bad. I miss hearing his voice on the telephone. We were getting to know each other all over again. It was like we were kids growing up together again.

My Angelo family lived over five hundred miles away. We only got to see each other once a year. But we were still close to one another.

Little by little I began to feel better. After nine days, they dismissed me from the hospital. I went home weak, feeling like I could lick the world.

Alas, three months later I contracted pneumonia again. I should have known by the way I was coughing that something was amiss. But, not wanting to go back to the hospital, I let it go too long without telling anyone that I was having problems.

This time I couldn't breathe. It was hard to get air into my lungs. I had to call Richard to come down and help me up the stairs. He came running down and literally pushed me up the stairs. While he was doing that, Angela called 911.

The firemen came pretty fast. Hooking me up to oxygen they carried me out to the ambulance, inserted the needle and hooked me up to an IV. Then they whisked me back to the hospital. Angela rode with us.

I was admitted a second time for pneumonia and had the same treatment that I had with the last bout. Same old, same old, but this time I was there for only six days.

When they sent me home after six days, I had to take several pills along with the steroids. It scared me because of the rise in blood sugar level, but I did what they told me to do and took the steroids.

From that time on, whenever I start to cough, pneumonia is in the back of my mind. Only now I don't hesitate to see the doctor as soon as possible.

He would take an x-ray and prescribe a prescription for an antibiotic that I could take without an allergic reaction, and a strong cough medicine. The remedy seemed to have worked, because it has been two years since I had another case of pneumonia.

However though, one night not too long ago, I woke up from a sound sleep and couldn't get any air. I struggled a few moments until I caught my breath again. I don't know why that happened but it was upsetting. I had such a fear of being put back in the hospital I didn't tell the doctor about this episode.

I think I've gotten a bit paranoid when it comes to doing all I can to stay away from the hospital and doctor appointments.

On the other hand, as of yet, I haven't figured out why that breathing incident happened.

Although I was diagnosed as being in remission at this time, Dr. Medathada informed me that I still had to have some tests done, and that I still had to see the other doctors every year to keep a check on it.

So, there it was, I still wasn't through running around town to doctor's offices. I learned later that it was not a bad thing, it was all good.

She advised me to take precautions when it comes to pneumonia. I had to wear a mask when I went shopping and to stay away from anyone that has a cold or the flu.

Now it may not sound like it, but that was good news. I could do it. That was duck soup for me.

It was all the other downers that sneaked into my life and made their way to the surface that I considered bad news. Subsequent to overcoming the bouts with pneumonia, I started to have a pain near my right hip. I had to see another doctor. Naturally, it had to be a specialist, so I went to see an orthopedic doctor named Justin D. Harris. He was young, and I felt confident being in his care. I liked him right away.

Whenever I am confronted with a new doctor, I have an instinct that tells me they are the one.

My summation is just that, but this is what I think. I like older doctors, for I think they have a lot of experience. Other times, I think if they are young they will be up on the latest procedures. Dr. Harris became another of my favorite doctors. I felt a connection with him.

Needless to say, after several tests and x-rays the doctor informed me that my hip was bone on bone and as time rolls on it could become quite painful.

For some reason, the words to a song ran through my mind, 'O Lord, won't you give me a Mercedes Benz?'

Chapter 9
Give Me A Break

Regrettably, I wasn't going to get a break.

After Dr. Harris told me the x-ray of my right hip was showing bone on bone, I had to figure out if I wanted to have a hip replacement. I couldn't stand the thought of living with that kind of pain and possibly not being able to walk, so I made the decision to have the hip surgery.

Now then, here I was in the midst of being excited that I was in remission, and I had to make another medical evaluation on the state of affairs confronting me.

First, I went to a class where they showed what the device looked like that they were going to implant in my hip area. It weighed five pounds and kind of reminded me of a stake. All I could think of was, oh brother, I am going to weigh five pounds more. That being said, here I go, off to the hospital for hip surgery. Ouch! It was not a pleasant time. Pain is not my friend.

When I woke up from surgery, I had on tight white stretch hose that go up to your knees. I had to wear them for six weeks to prevent blood clots.

The doctor's order was for me to get up the same day as surgery. I couldn't walk so they wheeled me into a rehabilitation room where other patients who'd had the same procedure done are waiting for the rest of us to join them, and we did light exercise together.

It's hard to believe that they release you from the hospital after three days. But they do. The doctor recommended that I should go to a rehabilitation facility.

In reality, I didn't want to go straight home this time, because not only did I hurt, I had to learn to walk all over again. Little did I know that I would be there for a whole month?

I was willing to go to Tabitha nursing home peacefully and do what I was told to regain the use of my body. I had to learn to live with the apparatus they put in my hip.

Golly sakes, to make matters worse, right after I woke up from the hip surgery, I came down with a bladder infection. I thought the infection might have come from the catheter they inserted in my bladder during surgery.

I don't know that for sure. I just know that it was awfully uncomfortable. I felt the urge to go to the bathroom every few minutes. It was painful.

Being the big baby that I am when it comes to pain and medicine, I called my family doctor and asked if he would prescribe something.

That was when I learned that I was now in the care of the staff doctor at Tabitha for my medical needs, and he couldn't prescribe anything.

Carrying myself through life I used to always say, "This, too, shall pass." Needless to say, eventually, it did pass, and my bladder got better, and I quit having to run to the bathroom every five minutes.

I was uncomfortable, but things were calming down. I went to rehab three times a day. I did all I was told and was always ready to go when the nurses came to put me in the wheelchair and wheel me down to the rehab room.

I was being such a show off. I wanted to be teacher's pet. Just kidding - I was doing a good job because of my competitive nature. I wanted to be the best I could be at what I was doing. I have this thing about me that wants to finish what I start.

The fact of the matter is, that it made me feel good to get along with the rehabilitation therapists. Some of them said I was one of their favorite patients. Although they may tell that to everyone, it put a smile on my face.

The exercises weren't hard but they weren't altogether painless. I worked at it. It made me sad to see the other older people in such pain. I'd sit in my wheelchair waiting my turn saying a prayer under my breath for the people who were moaning and suffering.

I had to remind myself that I was not a spring chicken. I was old. But it usually doesn't dawn on me. I try to live like I am younger than I really am. It doesn't always work out that way, but I try.

Forgetting that I am a senior, I never remember to ask for a senior citizens discount.

In reality, I didn't mind being at Tabitha nursing home. It was a new experience for me. I kind of liked being pampered and having help right there at my fingertips. I needed to learn so many things so I would know how to function once I was released.

Frankie lived close to the facility and she came to see me every day. Her boyfriend, Jaime, came to see me quite often too. He liked to take me for a ride in the wheelchair and down to the gift shop. We'd sit at one of the tables nearby and have a cup of coffee and shoot the breeze.

Angela and Megan came as often as they could. Sometimes they would bring Tobey with them. That was always a treat. He'd play with his toys and we'd get him snacks from the cafeteria.

Since I was always in the electric recliner resting my legs, Megan and Angela took turns taking a nap in my bed. It was a hoot to look over and see them sleeping. Sometimes they would stay and eat lunch with me. I ended up celebrating my birthday in the nursing home.

We all went to the cafeteria and had lunch, where everyone, including the residents that were sitting in the room, sang

'Happy Birthday' to me. It made me feel good that they were enjoying the festivities with us.

One of the nurses gave me a yummy decorated cupcake. Megan had her laptop with her and was Skyping with her fiancé, Mike King. The employees working in the lunchroom were getting interested in the fact that we were talking to a military man, and they wanted to talk to him, too. He was getting a kick out of talking to us as we were all vying for his attention at one time. It is such a nice thing that everyone loves to talk to the boys in the military. Mike was stationed in Qatar, which is near Afghanistan.

We considered him to be a hero. It was his second tour of duty. It is always such an honor to talk to the boys serving our country. He was about to become my grandson.

I saved the cupcake the nurse gave me and brought it back to my room where I intended to devour it later on. I was so tired I didn't get around to eating it, so I gave it to one of the gals that came in to take care of me.

All in all, it was a good birthday. I didn't mind that I celebrated it in the nursing home. It was my 'I'll try anything once' motto. I enjoyed it immensely.

The next day I had to make a trip to see Dr. Harris to have the surgery area checked on. I had to be wheeled into a van with a lift, then hauled to the doctor's office. One of the girls came with me. She wasn't able to stay with me until the appointment was over.

Megan met me there so I wouldn't have to face the doctor alone. I dislike it when I become anxious and I'm all alone. I wanted to have someone with me.

After a few minutes we were called into the other room where the doctor said I was coming along okay, and he would have me back in a week to take out the clamps.

Before leaving his office, we started to talk about other things. He got a kick out of the fact that I was an author. I told him that I would bring him a few of the books that were published while I was undergoing treatments.

Time moved along, and I was on the mend, when Mike, home on leave, and Megan took me back to the doctor to get the clamps out of my hip. Double ouch. Thank God another obstacle out of the way.

The month went by fast and it was soon time for me to go home. Angela was going to pick me up when she got off work. I was happy to be going home to see my family, my dog, and to sleep in my own bed.

The one thing that troubled me about going home was that I was worried about getting into the car. I practiced how to do it when I was in the rehabilitation room, but I was still apprehensive about it. You had to have your back end touch the car seat and sit then bring in one leg and then the other.

I had only been outside a few times in the last thirty days. It felt good to breathe in the fresh air.

It was a hot day. Bees were buzzing all around. I had to be careful and not try to outrun the bees like I usually do. I was still sore but doing so much better.

We arrived at our house. My great-grandson Tobey had covered the door with welcome home signs and pictures he had colored just for me.

The family was waiting in the front room to greet me as I walked through the door. Tobey was most excited to see me. He always called me Jo Jo. He wanted to give me a gift, so he wrapped some of his little toys up and gave them to me.

As the guest of honor, they ordered my favorite food, pizza. How wonderful to be home again - so why was I crying? I told the children they were tears of happiness. But that wasn't altogether true.

I can't put my finger on any one thing. It was a combination of things.

It came on me suddenly. I was overwhelmed and overcome not just with the love my family bestowed on me; it had to do with all that had gone on in the past four years. All the resolve I had portrayed to take everything one day at a time disappeared in an instant.

I acknowledged that one medical treatment after the other had finally taken their toll. I was totally worn out and tired. Of course, I knew it was ridiculous to simply think that I could sleep for a month. But that describes the feeling I had.

As hard as I tried to think forward, to cope and not think back, I'd still have flashbacks to the repulsive dreadfulness of the cancer and the treatments.

Thankfully, just as quickly as the feelings began, they disappeared. No matter how I tried though, they never fully left and at times they still haunt me.

Merely watching a movie or hearing something about cancer reminded me of certain things pertaining to what I lived through and what the chemicals did to my body.

Even the least little thing, like an announcement of a cancer walk, and I'd flash back to what cancer is and what it does. It never lasts long. I think it lurks around the corner. But then again, maybe mood swings are not always a bad thing.

Things settled down, I stopped crying, ate my pizza, and at last, at last, I got a good night's rest. The next morning, all was back to normal in my world. That is to say, whatever normal means. I just didn't know anymore.

Worried that I might fall, Richard walked in front of me as I walked down the thirteen stairs I had to use to get to my apartment. I couldn't wait to see my dog once again and sleep in my own room, in my own bed.

Going through the cancer treatments, it got harder and harder for me to take care of my spacious duplex. It was getting difficult to go up and down the stairs to let the dog out five to six times a day.

I loved my home. I thought of it as a perfect writer's castle. It was bright and sunny and peaceful. But, I finally had to admit that I wasn't able to take care of my home any more.

We decided it was time to move. I was still going through cancer treatments when Richard and Angela bought the house we are living in to this day. It is a beautiful home.

I liked the fact that I would have my own apartment. We felt the need to be in close proximity so they could keep a closer watch over me. I am a blessed woman.

The one thing my space didn't have was a kitchen. Richard designed one and had it put in for me. I felt a need to be as independent as I could be for the shape I was in. I couldn't stand the thought of being a burden to anyone. Besides, I like having my own space.

In rehabilitation, they taught me how to go up and down stairs carefully. I had to be very cautious about falling. They taught me to say, "up with the good, down with the bad." Meaning, use the good leg to go up the stairs and the bad leg to go down.

It has been two years since hip surgery. I still have to remind myself "up with the good, down with the bad", when I am faced with having to go up and down steps, no matter how many there are.

One day, when I was especially overtired, I fell. It wasn't on the stairs, it was after I had walked down the stairs and into my apartment.

I walked in the door and boom, there I was, lying on the floor. I couldn't get up. I crawled to the door and opened it.

Trying to be funny like the advertisement on TV for Life Alert I said, "Help, I've fallen and I can't get up."

Richard, Mike and Tobey came running down the stairs to check on me.

I said, "Clumsy me, I fell. I'm okay though; I just need help getting up."

After that fall, whenever I felt myself falling I tried to put the full weight of the fall on my left side, which was the opposite side of where I had the hip surgery.

Thankfully, I didn't hurt anything. I did end up going to the doctor to ask if he thought anything might have happened to my hip. The doctor said, "If anything were out of place, you'd be in so much pain you wouldn't be able to stand it."

As brave as I tried to act, after I fell, another fear set in. It was fear of falling. I began to baby my right leg and try to make sure I didn't put my full weight on it and try not to turn too fast. I make a point of not going outside when it is raining, snowing or icy. Right up to the time I had the hip surgery, it never entered my mind to be fearful about walking or falling.

After throwing caution to the wind and doing my own thing for so many years, I had to learn to adjust to living a certain way. Of course, throwing a prayer in there every day helps keep me going.

Chapter 10
The Angelos

Life goes on, and so did I. I continued going for the cancer tests, and each time I was told the same thing. I am in remission. Remission, what a beautiful word.

Each time I was told that I was in remission, I thanked God for his healing power. Hence, it was wonderful being able to wake up each morning to see another sunrise and sunset.

I witnessed and shared what I felt about God to all the doctors, nurses, and whoever would listen. I believe it is a miracle to continue to be on the face of the earth.

Although I acted exuberant and joyful about the medical report, in the back of my mind was the thought of cancer shooting its dangerous arrows my way again and again. It came to my mind after hearing stories of people in remission being stricken with the disease again and passing away.

Yet, I tried my darnedest to shake that thought, and continued to talk about God to most of the doctors and nurses that were open to whatever I said.

Some of them commented that they were believers and their faces lit up with the light of Christ when they said the name of Jesus. Which of course, put a smile on my face.

No matter how many times my thoughts flowed from joy to fear at the drop of a pin, I felt like God's hand was there, touching me throughout the entire history of my saga. No matter what I faced, I wasn't facing it alone.

During my down times I'd think of the scripture Hebrews 13:5b - 'I will never leave you, nor forsake you.'

Three of my brothers, Tony, Mike, and Sam, passed away from cancer complications. I also had two sisters-in-law, Janet and Cherie, that also died of cancer around twelve years ago. It was upsetting and heart-rending that so many in my family were dying of cancer.

At times I felt traumatized by the things they went through in their quest to submit to the cancer treatments. I'd think of what they experienced from beginning to end. It made me think that as bad as it was, what I suffered was not as harsh as what they endured.

My brothers and sisters and I lived miles away from one another, and it was hard to go see them often. But through the years we kept in touch.

It wasn't a big deal that in the old days, we sent letters in the mail using the United States postal service. That was our form of communication. I never dreamed I would come to love the days of watching for the mailman.

We also made telephone calls to keep in touch. We didn't call often, for way back then it was expensive to call long distance. You had to pay by the minute.

My brother Tony and his wife Barb, and my brother George and his wife Janet and their families lived in the Boston area. Joe and Cherie, Skeets and Bill, Sam and Liz, and my sister Antoinette lived in Illinois. Brother Mike lived in South Dakota, then he moved back to Illinois; brother Frank and his wife Dwayne (yes, Dwayne is female) live in Georgia.

Through the years, I only got to see some of them only a few times. Although we weren't close in miles, we were close in heart.

It was too hard for the entire family to get together all at one time. Everyone was busy working, raising children and trying to survive. I tried to make the trip back to my home state in Illinois once a year to see my mom and siblings that lived there. I also tried to meet at least once a year with my youngest brother, Frank, and his wife Dwayne. We started to meet in different states with other members of the family. Several times we met in California, Illinois, Boston and Tennessee.

It was always heart-warming and fun to see my brothers and sisters. I wished we could have been closer when we were growing up. It was after we got older that we got to know one another even more.

My father passed away forty years ago and my Mom passed away almost twenty years ago. I love my Angelo family.

When I think of my family, I think of what hard working people they were, how much they loved their families and took good care of them.

All in all, through the years quite a few members of my family passed away. Or as I like to say, left the face of the earth to fly with the angels.

Thinking of the Angelos, a flashback jars my memory. After I accepted Jesus as my savior I started to tell my family about my experience.

I'd go back home to see my brothers and sisters, Joe and Cherie, Bill and Skeets, Sam and Liz and their families, and my nieces and nephews along with other relatives. I'd talk about God to anyone that would listen and even to those who didn't.

On the other hand, after a while I thought I might be talking about God too much and it was a turn off, so I stopped doing it all the time. I settled down to chitchat about other things.

When Sam passed away, it affected me in a big way. He had been in remission for twelve years before the cancer took his life. He was fun to be around. He loved cooking and used to fix us the best corned beef and cabbage ever.

To this day on St. Patrick's Day my family has me make them corned beef and cabbage the same way Sam made it. It is an all-day venture that I don't mind doing, for it is a good memory of my brother.

Flashing back, I'll never forget when my younger brother Mike died. I was distraught. He was such a neat guy with a cool sense of humor.

123

Mike called me one evening and he said, "Josie, how come you never preach to me anymore?"

I said, "Oh, Mike, I stopped talking about Jesus because I thought I was bugging you."

Mike said, "No, you weren't bugging me. I want you to start preaching to me again."

I said, "Okay, Mike, let's pray right now."

And then, at that very moment we did pray together. Hallelujah, my brother Mike accepted Jesus right then and there. All we did was say a few words, 'Jesus forgive me for my sins, come live in my heart, and be Lord of my life'. Mike thanked me and asked me to keep talking about God. I was so happy after our conversation.

That was on a Sunday. My brother died two days later on the following Tuesday. The angels took him by the hand into the Promised Land. Wow, to pray with him at this crucial time was one of the highlights of my life.

Here I was thinking that I was being a pain in the behind. All the time he was listening and becoming a believer through the words he heard me speak.

I am no Bible scholar. I'm just a plain, uncomplicated believer in the words of God. When I got saved the salvation message of accepting Jesus as Lord of my life is the message I wanted to share with everyone.

I didn't doubt for one second that God was involved in the good news of Mike asking me to share Jesus with him. We may think we are not doing anything to glorify God in our daily lives, but maybe talking about him sometimes is a good thing after all. Even when someone says, 'Knock it off; I don't believe in God.' Just think, without realizing it we may be planting a seed. When we feel we have done nothing more than been a pain that was bugging them, someone else could come along and water that seed.

I am always and forever blessed by my brother Mike's words. I miss him so much. Here he was suffering from cancer, and he always worried about me, calling me every day to check up on me. What a guy. I love him.

My brother Tony died first, then Mike, then Sam, and then Joe. I was glad that Frankie and Jaime took me back to Illinois to see Sam while he was still alive. He passed away a month and a half later.

We didn't stay in his room very long, for he was so sick and so tired. But I felt I got to see him when it counted. When I asked Sam if he wanted to pray, I wasn't sure how he would react toward my gesture, but he grabbed my hand right away. I was so happy that Sam and his wife, Liz, and I had the opportunity to pray together.

When we were done praying they told me that their pastor, who was their mailman too, had prayed pretty much the same thing with them.

Years ago, when I learned that Sam liked reading the Bible, I set out to win a certain bible I had seen at the Seventh Day Adventist church revival that was taking place in Marysville, KS. They were going to give the Bible to the person who brought the most people to one of the services. I rounded everyone up that I could think of to come to that revival meeting with me. Voila, I won that Bible.

I am not a Seventh Day Adventist, but I am open to visiting other religions.

That year I was proud to hand Sam the family Bible I wanted to win so I could give it to him. I never dreamed how much Sam loved that Bible, and how he read it all the time.

Several years later, they had a house fire that burned their house to the ground. Naturally the Bible was burned to a cinder. Sam told me that he hated that his favorite Bible was destroyed by fire and asked if I could get him another one. I tried and couldn't.
I bought him other Bibles, but he never liked any of them the way he liked the Bible I won for him.

I called the Adventists and tried to find him one of the same Bibles that he liked so much. They didn't know what I was talking about.

There was none to be found. I really wanted to surprise him so much with a copy of that Bible, but I guess it was not meant to be.

The doctor said Sam's cancer was stage four. It was in his bones now and he had three months to live. In my heart I knew seeing him this time around would be the last time I'd see Sam alive. Rest in peace.

Sam's wife, Liz, is one of the most wonderful women I know. She is from Hungary. Sam married her when he was in the army stationed in Germany. They were young and in love. This is such an endearing story. The night Sam passed away he patted the bed for Liz to come sit by him. She got on the bed, put her arms around him and he passed away in her arms. This is a goose bump moment. They had been married fifty-eight years. They were still young at heart and still so in love.

In the past five years, I also lost a brother-in-law, Bill Jannie, and a niece, Jackie, and my own twenty-year-old grandson, Shane, as well.

One night, Shane was with two of his friends in a car that was speeding down the road. The car crashed into a tree, crushing my grandson to death.

His two friends were shaken up, but they lived through it. I am glad that they were okay. But I question, why did Shane have to die then and there, at that moment? I love that boy.

How do we live with this? But we did and we do. Although we grieve in our own personal way, I have to lean on God's everlasting love to give me the stamina to live from day to day, minute to minute, second to second.

It's not always easy to keep the faith and stay the course. I'm human; I do cry out and question why.

I have to chalk this up as another one of the worst days of my life, when his mother, Shelly called to tell me her son Shane was dead.

I could hardly stand the pain not only in her voice but also in my heart. All I could think of was, how could this be? He is just much too young to die.

When I called Joe and Shelly back the sadness in their voices crackled across the miles. Needless to say, losing their first - born son was a shock to their system. There are no words to describe how earth-shattering this is.

Shane worked alongside his dad in his dad's business. They shared so much together.

I went to the door to my apartment that leads to upstairs, crying out to Richard and Angela that Shane was dead.

The next day we were making arrangements to go to Tennessee to the funeral. I was supposed to ride with Frankie, and we were supposed to all leave at the same time of six a.m.

At the last minute, Frankie got sick, blacked out and fell to the floor. Jaime had to take her to the emergency room. She was not able to go to the funeral. Jamie assured me that he would take care of her. I ended up riding with Angela, Richard, Megan and Tobey.

Traveling the miles to Tennessee was the easy part. It was hard for me to get in and out of the van. I was still queasy and hurting from the cancer treatments and surgery.

Cancer never lets me forget that it was in my body. It has to rear its ugly head to let you know that it was part of your life. I hate cancer.

I didn't care what would have happened to me. I had to get to Joe and Shelly's house. We finally made it to their home.

Joe and Shelly had four of my grandchildren. I had not seen their new baby girl yet. Her name was Josie. I was honored they named her after me.

When we arrived in Tennessee and went into the house I thought Drenda and Chance looked as if they were in shock. They were trying to be brave. Yet, they were pale and quiet the whole time we were there.

I couldn't stand to see the pain in their father and mother's faces. As tears flowed down my cheeks, I reflected on the fact that Shane was no longer on the face of the earth.

He will never have the chance to play his guitar or marry and have children. I'd never be able to catch him on messenger again when he was supposed to be in bed because he had to get up early for school. I loved catching him on the computer when he thought he wouldn't get caught being up so late. He had the most wonderful sense of humor. I loved talking to him. He used to call me on the phone and he got a kick out of me because when we first started talking, I'd think I was talking to his dad.

He'd giggle and say, "Grandma, this is me, Shane."

It was over and we had to accept it as a fact and try to live with the tragedy. Sounds easy to say, but so hard to do, and somehow, we have to learn to muddle through.

One member of my family died each year for the past five years. Whether it was from cancer or something else, it was heart breaking and weighed heavily on my heart.

It felt gloomy that I wasn't able to attend several of the family funerals. Either they lived too far away or I wasn't feeling good, or I had no one to take me there.

Somehow the beat goes on, and through the sadness and the grief we strive to do the best we can.

Not knowing why things happen the way they do, I've pondered on: Why am I still here and they are gone? Why was I ever born? What purpose do I have here? What is my destiny? The questions haunt me every now and then. I am not wise enough to know. I don't have all the answers.

All I deem for certain about what they went through in passing away is that my loved ones are flying with the angels now. Standing before the throne of God praising and worshipping God the Father and Jesus the Holy Son.

That should have been enough for me to accept, but each time I had to face yet another tragedy, I wondered why.

Being human, I question things all the time. I dissect and analyze and ponder on all that takes place in this lifetime, yet realize that I merely need to keep the faith, to trust in God no matter what happens. When I falter, I pray, "God help me have faith; help my unbelief."

I wrote a poem for a two-year-old little boy, Cameron, who died of leukemia several years ago.

After I wrote the poem I wondered if the words could help comfort others who had suffered the loss of a loved one. I began to send the poem to those who lost a loved one. People began to read the poem at the funerals. Therefore, hoping it ministers to someone, I am sharing it with you all. It is titled:

Flutter Of Angel Wings

I heard the flutter of angel wings,
Its sound arose when you were near.
Knowing you was such a thrill,
It's hard to describe the way I feel

When I hear the wind blow, or smell a rose,
The wisp of angel wings from above
Remind me of how much you were loved.

One minute you were here,
The next you were gone.
Flying with the angels,

131

You're going to live on.
I'll keep singing you
A sweet lullaby song
Long after you are gone.
Now you're flying with the angels in the sky,
Whispering sounds of God's love wave by.
I miss your smiling face,
Your brave countenance,
The days we spent together
Were a gift from above.
As pure as a snow-white dove.

I heard the flutter of angel wings
When they took you by the hand
Into the Promised Land,
Where there is no more crying, no dying,
No sadness, no more pain.
There is only the sound of rejoicing and praise.

Now you're face to face with the most high God.
The flutter of Angel wings fills the air.
Heavenly joy is everywhere.
One day we will be reunited.

Living in the kingdom for all eternity,
Forever and ever
With Jesus Our King.

How great it will be
When we see you again.
Feel the love –
God is truly our friend.

I love reading poetry and I love writing it. Sometimes I have doubts as to whether the poems I write are good enough to share with others.

Or, maybe it is a case of beauty is in the eye of the beholder.

Chapter 11
Home Sweet Home

Ah, at last, home sweet home. After the nursing home, surgery and rehab were behind me, it was time to concentrate on what I wanted to accomplish. It had been a long hard haul but I was ready to do my own thing.

It's not like I could run around the block. I have to watch where I walk. I have a limp and can't walk without a cane, but that is no big thing.

Just being able to walk is a gift. But surely there must be something constructive that I could do at this time.

I had to focus on the fact that not all the problems I encounter are from the hip surgery, some of them are from the after-effects of the chemo treatments. Chemo makes my feet feel as if they are asleep, like pins and needles.

I have three fingers on my right hand that feel that way all the time, too. When it gets cold, I have to wear a glove, even in the house, for the cold makes it ache even more. I sum it all up to just another day in the Butler household.

Several years ago, I started to write several stories and a screenplay, but I had to put them on hold. So much was going on all the time. One thing I wanted to do was to go back and finish writing those stories.

Richard and Angela had their cross to bear with some physical problems, and then Megan contracted POTS (postural orthostatic tachycardia syndrome) while she was pregnant, which is a story unto itself.

Angela takes everything on and confronts it, finding solutions for everyone. I wonder if she realizes what an amazing and wonderful person she is; that she has a right to live her life the way she wants to live it and do her own thing, so to speak.

Like everyone else, she gets tired and would like things to calm down, but they haven't. She is like the energizer bunny that just keeps going and going.

However, I worry about her. No one can take everything on by themselves and yet, she is always the first to be there for others. Today, she left work to pick up some medicine for me, then went right back to work. That is the kind of heart she has.

Frankie and Megan were there to help me through tough times, too, along with Richard and Mike. I loved it when Frankie cooked for me. Joe used to call a lot and send me much-needed money.

The children all helped in their own ways. It was fantastic to have my whole family rally around me. We loved being together all at one time. I was grateful to all of them for being by my side when I needed them to rally around me.

But time had a way of zooming by and getting away from us. Everyone became busier and busier. I used to speculate on whatever happened to the lazy days we spent together? I miss the days where we just sat around shooting the bull. There just didn't seem to be any time left in the day to enjoy the same things we did just a few years ago. Finding time just to sit back and plainly take it easy was getting harder and harder to do.

Seems like one minute it is December and the next it is July. I thought it was because I was getting old, but even the young people feel it and talk about it.

I didn't have to wait long to figure out what I was going to do after recouping from my hip surgery.

Megan and Mike got married and she became pregnant. They wanted to have a baby girl in the worst way. A few months into the pregnancy Megan began to spin out. She became very ill. She had a hard time catching her breath, her heartbeat became irregular and she got dizzy and fainted.

The first time it happened, we were on our way to buy her dad a gift at a Harley Davidson store not too far from home. She said, "Josie, I'm afraid. I am really dizzy."

"Park the car and we will sit in it a while until you get your bearings," I replied.

She parked the car by the curb on the street we were driving on and we sat and rested awhile. After she caught her breath, she drove to the Harley store. I had her sit in the car while I went in. After I got back to the car she drove us back to my house.

Megan parked the car in our driveway, and that was the end of her driving days for around four years. Unfortunately, from that moment on, she was afraid to be alone for one moment. Each morning around six a.m. Mike dropped Megan and Tobey off at her dad and mom's house while he went to work. She knew that with me here she wouldn't have to be alone. She could call me anytime and I would go upstairs and sit with her.

Not knowing what was going on with her, we were both sad and frustrated at the same time. Her obstetrician at the time acted like nothing was wrong.

She ended up going to numerous doctors but to no avail. The condition persisted and we didn't have any answers.

She lost thirty pounds in a few weeks. This certain doctor showed no empathy and did nothing to help her or find out what was going on.

As time moved on she was taken to the ER numerous times during the course of her pregnancy. She changed doctors several times.

Megan finally found a doctor that was sympathetic toward her condition and she helped get her through her pregnancy and safely to childbirth.

The time came and she had a beautiful baby girl, Perry Antoinette King. We are all so crazy about her and her brother Tobey, who is seven years old at this time. We thought after she had the baby that she would feel better. But that didn't happen.

I stayed at their house for a week when she came home from the hospital, for she still couldn't do anything without being dizzy. She could hardly make it to the bathroom without falling. She wasn't home long before she took another fall. That pierced my heart. I couldn't stand to see her so sick.

Megan's progress consisted of her being able to use a walker to go to doctor's appointments. She used to use the walker like a wheel chair, sitting in it backwards and using her feet to push it to where she needed to go in the house.

She was in bed most of the time. If we put the baby on the bed with her she was able to change her diaper and feed her.

When Perry turned one year old on July 30th, Megan was still not quite able to do things for herself. She still suffered with being lightheaded, weak, sick, had heart palpitations and was able to walk without aid or be left alone.

It was at this point that Megan's friend told a local TV station about her physical problems and her dilemma of having no insurance. The doctor bills were accumulating and piling high. Megan's dilemma interested the TV station, and they did a story featuring Megan, Mike, Tobey and Perry on one of the shows. The station took up a collection to send her to Dallas, Texas to a POTS clinic that specializes in that type of disease.

A local bar held a silent auction and gave her the proceeds. The church took up a collection and did all they could to help the family. Some of her friends used to come by with food and stayed to help watch over the baby. It was heartwarming and awesome to see the way the town stood behind her, to see so many people come to her aid.

Praise God, with the donations that came in from the various places they had enough money to go to the clinic and were soon on their way to Dallas. We were all so thankful and hopeful.

During this time, I continued to help with the baby and Tobey. We hired someone to watch Perry in the morning a few days a week. Then I took over. When Grandpa Richard and Grandma Angela came home from work, they relieved me. We had a system going on and it worked out fine.

Megan and Mike were at the clinic for two weeks, but soon enough they were back home from Dallas. We learned that it is a slow process, and she is still on a treatment program, but still has the same symptoms.

She ended up going to three more clinics that were out of town. But yet, she still suffered from the disease and still wasn't able to do very much and tries to get through the day the best she can.

I was thankful that I felt well enough to help care for and cook for Megan and the children.

I don't want to be taken for a martyr; I just want to do what I can for as long as I can to help the children.

Although, I have to admit, it isn't easy for me to take care of things for more than four to five hours in a day. I start to lose my strength and wear down. On the other hand, it is a blessing to be able to be there for my family. It is amazing how the adrenalin works to keep you going when you need it.

When Mike and Megan got back from Texas, the first clinic she went to, I learned that she still needed me to help them. Megan had a full day of exercises to do, and it was still hard for her to do anything or to leave the house.

I started to go over to her house. Angela or Richard used to drive me there at six-thirty a.m. so Mike could leave for work. When he came home from work around five p.m., he helped Megan, Tobey and Perry into the car and took me home, then he took Megan to doctor appointments. At times Richard and Angela came by to take me home.

We all pulled together and we made it work for a while. I thank God for giving us all strength to get through the day. However, after three months of getting up with the chickens and being away from home, I was wearing down. Once again, we switched houses and the children and Megan began to come to my house again, for it was easier for me to take care of them from my home.

At this time, Tobey is in school all day and Perry goes to daycare two days a week. So that frees up some time for me to do the things I like to do, and of course catch up on rest.

Even though my mind thinks like a young person, my body gives out and I need a nap. However, when I think of it, when I was young I liked taking a nap, especially on Sunday. Nevertheless, I wouldn't change a thing. I love hanging out with my family. My children, my grandchildren and my great-grandchildren are the love of my life.

My great-grandson Tobey and I are already good friends. Now I'm having fun becoming good friends with Perry. I love being friends with my children, for it brings us even closer.

The family continues to pray that Megan will get her strength and stamina back and that she will be made whole again.

We did so many things together, and she was such fun. She was always vibrant and outgoing. She loved taking her son to school and afterward, picking him up from school, working at her spa, going shopping, out to eat and all the things young people love to do.

She was so beautiful, inside and out. I couldn't stand to see her sick and helpless.

The good news is that a doctor that saw the TV show where Megan was featured called her on the phone and told her he wanted to help her. His name is Dr. Hruska. He did just what he said; he helped her overcome and be able to function again.

We learned from Dr. Hruska that what Megan was suffering from was something called Lyme disease, and that snowballed into what is called POTS.

The doctor worked long and hard with her. He was so gentle with her, and slowly but surely, she was able to do little things for herself and her family. She didn't have to use the walker anymore. It took around four-and-a-half years before she fully recovered the full use of her body.

My prayer practitioner, Miles, was also on the scene, praying for her and encouraging her on the telephone.

At this particular time, she takes care of her home, husband and children on her own. She is doing so many things now, I can't keep up with her. She has even opened up a beauty spa.

God is so good. His mercy endures forever.

She still has to be careful and not overdo it. She has Mike to help her in that area. I think Mike is related to Superman. He was taking care of his little family, working and going to school. He was running errands and he did the shopping. He was a wonderful carpenter and in between everything else he would take on building a house project.

Like the old saying goes, 'When life has a way of throwing lemons, we have to learn how to make lemonade.' Not an original saying, but at times it rings true.

I'm not relating anything new when I say that we all know how precious time is. Or when we say that time is the most valuable commodity ever, for you can't buy back time.

When I heard that my sister-in-law Cherie had brain cancer, I called her on the telephone. Even though she knew she didn't have long to live, her voice had a lilting ring to it. I could envision that her countenance sounded beautiful, and her attitude sounded heartfelt.

During the course of our conversation, in saying goodbye to one another, she said, "Josie, get a paper and pencil and write down these words:

"If you were a trillionaire you can't buy back yesterday. No one has a guarantee. Yesterday is gone. Tomorrow may never come. So, live today to its fullest, as though it were your last minute, with the people you love. Today is light and sunshine. That's the day you walk with a smile. Let nobody hurt or bother you."

"Those words are enchanting," I said.

Cherie said, "Jesus told me that I am going to heaven. He is building me a mansion and I will be living in it soon."

Wow! was the only thing I could think of to say after I realized that she had accepted her destiny without a word of complaint. Her voice sounded like it was filled with happiness. That was awesome. She is sensational.

I believe God speaks to us in many ways. I admit I have been skeptical when someone tells me God spoke to him or her in an audible voice. But in Cherie's case, I have no doubt that Jesus did actually speak those comforting words to her.

The second she told me what Jesus said to her, I thought of the scripture in John chapter 14, verse 1. "Let not your heart be troubled: ye believe in God, believe also in me. In my Father's house are many mansions: if it were not so, I would have told you. I go to prepare a place for you."

I thought of it as confirmation that Jesus did indeed speak to Cherie.

I had written a song for Christmas that I wanted to play on the piano and sing to her, so I took the phone with me and set it on the piano and proceeded to play and sing the song. I said, "Cherie, I don't know why the particular lyrics and melody came to me."

Cherie was crying when she said, "I believe you wrote the song especially for me."

I said, "Yes, I believe that is the reason I wrote it, for sure."

With a happy tone in her voice Cherie said, "I love Christmas time. I am so happy to have my entire family all around me."

It was hard to believe she was whisked into heaven just a few weeks after we talked on the telephone.

I sent a copy of the words she had told me to write down to her husband. He had them engraved in gold on a plate that he hung on his bedroom wall.

Thinking of her words, I thought of the statement that says we can't buy back even the last second of time that passed us by. Writing my story, I didn't want it to sound like a downer. All the same, sometimes I think about all those I knew that had cancer treatments and were in remission, and are no longer alive, and it makes me wonder.

Why does cancer even get another chance to come back? I know there are stories out there where cancer didn't come back, but it bothers me when I hear that it does.

One can't help but have flashbacks into their experience with cancer or anything else life-threatening. This holds true to whatever experience one has had with life's up and downs in general.

I can't help it; sometimes I think of it happening to me, and I cringe from it. Then again, none of us really knows how much time we have.

Psalm 139, verses 15-16 say: "My frame was not hidden from you, when I was made in secret, and skillfully wrought in the lowest parts of the earth. Your eyes saw my substance being yet unformed. And in your book, they all were written, the days fashioned for me, when as yet there were none of them."

Believing that God is with us in everything we go through, during the entire ordeal of fighting cancer, an actress, Lydia Cornell, became one of my dearest friends. She starred in the sitcom, "Too Close For Comfort."

We met on the internet after I found her e-mail address on a list of addresses some one sent me, so I wrote to her. She wrote me back, and from then on, we kept in touch and continue to do so. She called and prayed with me so many times. She had health practitioners pray for me and call and encourage me, too.

As I battled cancer, one of the highlights of my life was when Lydia interviewed me on her radio show with Doug Basham. Although I was an unknown author, her interview turned the audience's attention to my writing.

She loved the books I wrote, titled, "Awesome Adventures of Frankie Stargazer" and, "Frankie Stargazer's Ultimate Battle," and also the screenplay titled, "Frankie Stargazer and The Power." I have hopes that she will one day direct and produce the screenplay into a movie for all to enjoy.

If not for God's destiny, how else could a famous, beautiful actress who lives in California and me, a Nebraskan, an unknown author and homemaker who rarely leaves her home, come to know one another so well?

The first time we met, we found that we both had Jesus Christ as Lord of our lives. Immediately we had a common spiritual bond; we were sisters in the Lord. I felt as close to Lydia as if I had known her all my life.

I wonder if she will ever know how much her telephone calls meant to me. She is so encouraging and loving. She called me throughout all the physical ordeals I endured during the last seven years.

If I wasn't home, she left the longest, sweetest messages on my answering machine. The words were so endearing that I tried to tape them on a small recorder so I could hear them again. She even took time to call me while I was in the hospital.
We still call one another. Each call is enjoyable and full of mutual love for God and for each other.

I think of her as an angel on earth. She has helped so many people in her life. She helps abused women and the homeless and does so many other charitable acts of love to help those in need.

Lydia is like one of the family. She holds my heart, too. I will forever and always think of her as one of my best friends. I am so blessed and thankful that Lydia came into my life. She puts a smile on my face.

Thanks to Lewis Hunter, I'd also like to say that the screenplay mentioned above was the first time I'd ever written a screenplay. I asked Lewis, who happens to be the author of Screenwriting 434 and a retired professor from UCLA, if he would write the screenplay for me.

Lewis said, "Josie, you are an excellent writer; you can write it yourself. You write it and I will check it out when you're finished."

So, there I was, challenged to do something I'd never done before. Needless to say, that didn't stop me. I looked at the format of how others wrote a screenplay, and I was off and running until I finished it.

I'm not saying I didn't make mistakes, but I did learn that people rewrite screenplays right up to the very last word.

Lewis is such a good soul. He mentored me and helped me to have the confidence to keep writing. I began to market myself. Eventually I met people interested in producing "Awesome Adventures of Frankie Stargazer."

During the course of this time, I would like to make mention of a producer I met named Mario Domina. In a roundabout way I met his mother, too. He took such good care of her in the most loving way.

I loved hearing the news about how his mother was doing. It was so endearing. I felt so close to her, I kind of adopted her as my own mom.

Over the years, Mario and I became good friends and are still in touch with one another. He taught me so much and gave me such good advice.

He introduced me to several people in the film industry and again, I was off and running, jumping at the opportunity to have my screenplay accepted.

At this time, I have a director, a producer and a team that we call the 'Frankie Stargazer team,' trying to move forward with the screenplay.

I hope it makes it to the big screen, but we shall see.

It takes vision, time and money, and oh, so much more. I still don't know exactly what all it takes to get to the end. I am thankful to the people who joined the team.

My family gets a kick out of the fact that I meet so many people in the movie-making business just sitting in my home. I feel fortunate that my bedroom is quite large, so that we made it into an office, too. I call it my bedroom/office hideaway.

Chapter 12
Yay God, Thanks

I have doubts, fears, and everything is not peaches and cream in my life. I have the same ups and downs and stress to deal with as most do.

The first words I say when I wake up in the morning are, "God give me the energy I need to get through this day." I know that if I don't pray for God's healing touch of strength that I am not going to make it.

Shortly after cancer treatments, pneumonia and the hip replacement I resented not having the strength, the time or the concentration to write on my stories and screenplays.

It was discouraging not to be able to market and have the stories that I wrote published as fast as I wanted. Or that it took so many steps for a movie to be developed. Energy or no energy, I had to be more patient.

After I quit having a pity party about what I wanted to do, I began to see the importance of what God wants me to do. To see what is significant in life, what has meaning and what is God-given. At this point, I couldn't look back, for I needed to give my ability and time to helping my grandchildren.

As the fog began to clear from my thoughts, I realized and grasped the fact that the most important event on earth after God, is family. Having a family is not a hardship; it is a blessing. It is a blessing from our heavenly father, God. It is what we do with God's blessings that matter.

As I told my family and friends more than once, I don't mean to preach, but when I hear of something that pertains to a certain subject, I can't help it. At times I just have to relate what I see and hear in God's word.

I'm aware of the fact that we don't all believe the same way, that we worship differently. The teachings and theology are different in the many diverse religions and teachings.

What I've shared throughout my story is what's in my heart. If I claim to be a Christian, then I should be obedient to the Lord and let my actions show that I love him and want to live a righteous life.

Someone once asked me, "You believe in God, but do you believe him?" That got me to thinking about my walk with God. I know I am not a goody two-shoes. I am not an angel. Sometimes I mess up big time. I falter and I slip, but I want to keep my eyes on the prize.

I can't help it if it turns anyone off.

I'm going to do whatever it takes to try the best I can to be faithful to the Almighty. No matter what happens, I'll keep pressing on.

I might add that I have a problem with trust. Our society is such that I don't trust certain people or certain things that confront my daily life.

As time went by the Bible became the one book I trusted and turned to for guidance and peace. I learned that the words in the Bible were the way to live life and the key to everlasting eternal life.

I rejoice at the thought of being redeemed and reunited with my loved ones who are in heaven today.

One day when I was listening to someone talk about a dysfunctional family, it got me to thinking about the way my brothers, sisters and I were raised.

My dad came from Italy and couldn't write or speak English very well. I believe we would have had a childhood that would have been labeled dysfunctional, but we never heard the word. Even though we were poor, we didn't think that anything in our life was unusual. We felt we had all we needed. We just accepted who we were and lived our lives the best we could. We loved one another, and that is what mattered.

After I had my own experiences in life I began to lose the trust that innocently graced me most of my life. I blindly trusted everyone. I would have been labeled gullible and naive. I tried to see the good in everything and everybody, but after an abundance of trial and error, I started to think that it is not humanly possible to trust just anyone ever again. I had to go back to the very beginning and teach myself all over again how to trust and who to trust.

The first thing I began to trust in again was God as my heavenly father. I accept through trust that he is the 'Everlasting Father' who was there for me even when I felt he wasn't.

I learned that having a relationship with God should be in the same manner that I have with my family, to always speak to God and go to him for answers, blessings, love and other life experiences, to talk to him in the same way I would talk to my family and friends. Just talking to God one on one taught me to have a rapport with him. I wasn't into religion. I was into relationship.

To God be the glory for the great things he has done.

To me, the words "When It Rings True" means more than a title. I think of it as a way of life. When cancer or any other disease or sickness comes to your door and starts to ring the bell, it is time to fight.

Fight for the right to be here. Fight for the right to attain the best medical treatment, whether you have insurance or not. It is all a battle. But it can be an uphill battle.

Being a warrior is more than a word; it is a state of mind. Warrior is climbing the ladder of life to the top and never giving up. Anyway, that's what I think a warrior is.

Once I became a cancer survivor, I started to think of myself as a cancer warrior, someone that stands above the world with a sword in my hand.

I don't think I would have made it without the will to want to live and be with my children, grandchildren and great-grandchildren.

On my last appointment to my oncologist, Dr. Medathada said, "Josie, you have reached the five-year mark. You don't have to come see me anymore unless you have problems. Isn't that wonderful? Remember, you told me your God was healing you. And you are still in remission."

I said, "So you are cutting me loose then?"

"Yes," she replied.

I said, "Thank you for everything, doctor. Couldn't have done it without you."

We gave each other a big hug and said goodbye.

As happy as I was that it was one less doctor I would have to see during the year, it also made me sad that I wouldn't be seeing her anymore.

All things do come to an end, and in this case, I hope it is the end of cancer being in my back yard.

Thanks, father God. My life is in your hands.

If I touched just one heart, if my words could bring just one person to know Jesus as their Lord and Savior, taking the time to write this story will have been meaningful. It will have been worth it.

I tried to write who I am as a person and who I am in the love of our Lord Jesus Christ, the King of kings.

I rejoice that Jesus is our savior and redeemer, that he gave his life, that he shed his blood on a cross so we could have eternal life and be reunited with our loved ones. I will see my family and friends once again for all eternity.

Before I accepted Jesus as number one in my life, I thought the salvation message was something complex. I thought we had to do a certain ritual. But I learned that is not the case. Actually, it turned out to be so simple and easy. I learned that all one has to do to be saved is to say: "Jesus forgive me for my sins. I believe you are the Son of God. Come live in my heart and be number one in my life."

Okay, so there I go preaching again. Oh well, what more can I say, for that is what is in my heart.

Sometimes things don't just happen; they happen for a reason. I was blessed to have been able to pray that very prayer with my brothers Mike, Sam, Joe, and my sister Antoinette before they passed on to fly with the angels. I miss all of them so much. I miss hearing their voices on the telephone. At times we talked for an hour or so. Thanks for the memories.

John, chapter 3, verse 16: "For God so loved the world that He gave His only begotten Son, that whoever believes in Him should not perish but have everlasting life."

Isaiah, chapter 12, verse 2 – 5: "Behold, God *is* my salvation, I will trust and not be afraid; 'For YAH, the LORD, *is* my strength and song; He also has become my salvation.' Therefore with joy you will draw water from the wells of salvation. And in that day you will say: "Praise the LORD, call upon His name; declare His deeds among the peoples, make mention that His name is exalted. Sing to the LORD, for He has done excellent things; this *is* known in all the earth."

Revelation 21:3-4: "And I heard a loud voice from heaven saying, 'Behold, the tabernacle of God *is* with men, and He will dwell with them, and they shall be His people. God Himself will be with them *and be* their God. And God will wipe away every tear from their eyes; there shall be no more death, nor sorrow, nor crying. There shall be no more pain, for the former things have passed away.' "

Luke 2:14: "Glory to God in the highest, and on earth peace, goodwill toward men!"

Bible scriptures are from "The New King James Version" by Thomas Nelson Publishers, Nashville.

www.ingramcontent.com/pod-product-compliance
Lightning Source LLC
Chambersburg PA
CBHW032036040426
42449CB00007B/904